Wild Stillness

A Journey into Mindfulness, Creativity, and the Sacred Wisdom of Nature

Offering 108 nature-based mindful practices.

Jan Carey

Centre for Mindful Education

© 2025 Jan Carey
Published by Centre for Mindful Education Pty Ltd
www.centreformindfuleducation.com.au

All rights reserved.

No part of this publication may be reproduced, stored in a retrieval system, or transmitted in any form or by any means—electronic, mechanical, photocopying, recording, or otherwise—without the prior written permission of the copyright holder, except for brief quotations used in reviews or scholarly works.

First published in Australia in 2025
ISBN:978-0-6452090-9-9

The moral rights of the author have been asserted.

National Library of Australia Cataloguing-in-Publication entry

Carey, Jan, 2025-, author.
Wild stillness :A Journey into Mindfulness, Creativity, and the Sacred Wisdom of Nature'/ Jan Carey.
ISBN: 978-0-6452090-9-9

Mindfulness—Practice. | Nature—Spiritual aspects. | Meditation—Therapeutic use. | Outdoor education—Activity programs. | Creative expression—Spirituality. | Self-development—Mindfulness practices.
158.1

Every effort has been made to trace copyright holders and obtain permission for any material reproduced in this book. The author and publisher welcome information that would correct any errors or omissions.

Contents

Introduction to Wild Stillness	5
Returning to Presence	15
Breathing with the Earth	31
Open Your Heart to the Wild	47
Awaken Your Senses	65
Create with the Land	81
Storytelling with Nature	105
Leaving No Trace	121
Sacred Earth, Sacred Self	137
Giving Back to the Earth	159
Your Wild Stillness Journey	169
Index of Practices	176
About the Author	180

Dedication

To
Sri Sakthi Amma Narayani,
my Beloved Guru,

Your grace is the flame that lit the stillness within me.
Your presence, the mirror through which I remembered who I truly am.

In the quiet of nature and the silence of breath,
your teachings echo—softly, powerfully, unmistakably.

May this offering born of earth and spirit,
rest humbly at your lotus feet
and carry forward even a whisper of your light.

Introduction

Wild Stillness

*Under a vaulted sky of tender blue,
among ancient trees that whisper secrets,
I step into a gentle realm
where the pulse of the earth and my own heartbeat merge.*

*In the quiet chorus of rustling leaves,
each breath becomes a hymn of presence,
a soft invitation to be fully alive
in the vast unfolding mystery of now.*

*In Wild Stillness, every whisper of the wind,
every gentle murmur of the earth,
echoes a truth:
we are all connected—each a vital note
in the symphony of life.*

Welcome to Wild Stillness

There is a quiet place within you—where the stillness of your being meets the wildness of the world. You have known it before, perhaps in a fleeting moment: standing beneath a sky full of stars, feeling the hush of the forest at dawn, watching the wind move through the trees as if whispering a language just beyond reach. This place, this sense of deep belonging and presence, is what *Wild Stillness* is about.

Wild Stillness is both a practice and a way of seeing the world. It is the stillness of presence—the ability to slow down, notice, and truly be where you are. And it is the wildness of nature—raw, untamed, ever-changing, and deeply alive. When these two meet, something profound happens. We begin to feel the land not just as something outside of us, but as something we are part of. We awaken to the rhythms of the earth, the language of the wind, the quiet teachings of trees and rivers. We remember that we are not separate from nature, but woven into its very fabric.

This book is an invitation. A journey into connection—connection with yourself, with nature, and with the quiet wisdom that lives in both. It is not about learning something new, but about remembering something ancient. A way of being that has always been within you, waiting to be reclaimed.

The practices in Wild Stillness do not tell you what to think or how to feel. Instead, they are gentle invitations to explore mindfulness, creativity, and connection in the natural world. Some will be simple, some will stretch you in new ways, all are meant to be approached with curiosity, playfulness, and an open heart.

More Than Just Being in Nature

Have you ever gone for a walk and suddenly realised you don't actually remember getting there? Your body moved through the landscape, but your mind was somewhere else—lost in thought, replaying conversations, worrying about things that haven't happened yet. You were in nature, but you weren't *with* it. The birds sang, the wind moved through the trees, the light shifted across the earth, but none of it truly reached you. You were physically present, but disconnected.

This kind of time in nature can still offer benefits—it gives us fresh air, movement, a break from screens—but when we remain in our heads, it does little to nourish us on a deeper level. We might return home feeling exactly the same as when we left.

Now imagine another kind of walk. One where you step into nature and let yourself *arrive* fully. You notice the way your breath moves in rhythm with your steps. You feel the texture of the earth beneath your feet. You inhale the scent of damp leaves, listen to the distant call of a bird, watch sunlight flickering through the trees. You don't rush. You don't analyse. You simply *experience*. This is more than just being in nature—it is being *with* nature. And in this way, nature gives back to you. Your nervous system calms. Your mind settles. Your heart opens. You begin to feel more connected—not only to the earth but to yourself.

Nature Practices in Ancient Wisdom

Long before modern mindfulness or wellness practices existed, ancient cultures around the world lived in *deep, reciprocal relationship* with the natural world. Nature was not something to escape to on weekends – it was home, healer, teacher, and temple. These traditions didn't separate spirituality, wellbeing, and the land. In Indigenous Australian cultures, deep connection to *Country* forms the heart of wellbeing. The land is alive with spirit and story. To walk mindfully, listen to the wind, observe the cycles, or follow a songline is to stay connected—to self, to ancestors, and to the sacred web of life.

In Vedic and yogic traditions of India, the five elements—earth, water, fire, air, and space—are seen as both physical and spiritual forces. Practices like breath awareness (*pranayama*), meditation, and rituals honour these elements within and around us, fostering inner balance and a sense of unity with all life.

In Taoism, living in harmony with the *Tao* (the Way) means observing and flowing with the rhythms of nature—following the changing seasons, honouring water's softness, and finding strength in stillness. Presence with nature was a path to inner peace and longevity.

In Celtic and Druidic traditions, the forest was sacred ground. Trees were guardians of wisdom, stones held memory, and the natural world pulsed with life force. Seasonal rituals and storytelling kept people aligned with the cycles of the earth and their own inner rhythms.

These ancient pathways remind us that nature connection is not a new idea—it is something *we are remembering*. They are a way of living that honours the earth, nourishes the soul, and brings us home to ourselves.

Nature Practices in Modern Times

Today, we have many modern-day pathways that guide us back into connection with the natural world. These approaches offer gentle and accessible ways of remembering our relationship with nature.

Forest therapy and forest bathing (Shinrin-Yoku, originating in Japan) are practices that invite us to spend slow, intentional time immersed in nature—breathing in its scents, listening to its quiet rhythms, and allowing our nervous system to settle into harmony with the land.

Eco-spirituality takes this further, recognising the earth as not only alive but sacred. It invites us to see that every stone, river, and leaf carries a kind of wisdom—if we are willing to listen.

Mindfulness-based practices have long held nature as a powerful ally. Mindfulness asks us to be fully here, to notice the details, to return again and again to this moment. And where better to practice presence than in the living classroom of the natural world?

In truth, these pathways all echo the wisdom of ancient traditions. Across cultures, our ancestors lived in deep reverence for the land. They knew that stillness under a tree, the rhythm of breath in the wind, and the sacredness of water were not ideas—they were ways of life.

Wild Stillness gently bridges these worlds: the old and the new, the ancient and the emerging. You don't need to belong to a tradition to benefit from this journey. What matters most is your willingness to return to presence, to listen, and to let the natural world guide you home.

The Journey of Wild Stillness

This book is a progression—a quiet unfolding, a gentle deepening, a journey that mirrors the natural rhythms of growth. Each chapter builds upon the one before it inviting you to move from outer awareness to inner stillness, from observing the world to feeling your place within it. You begin with the foundational practices of presence and breath, learning to ground yourself and return to the moment. From there, you open the heart, awaken the senses, and step into creative expression with the land.

This path is not a checklist, and there's no need to rush. Each chapter contains its own energy, its own lessons, its own gifts. Some you may linger in, others you may return to again and again. The practices are there to guide you, but you are the guide of your own experience.

To truly feel the essence of Wild Stillness, it's best to move through the book in order—letting yourself grow into each practice, letting it settle, letting it change you from the inside out. There's no timeline for this. No pressure. Only a quiet sense of readiness that will arise when the next step is calling. Trust that. Trust yourself.

There are 108 nature-based mindful practices included in the book. The first three chapters are the **core of wild stillness living**, the essential skills that will shape how you experience the world, nature, and yourself.

Chapter 1. Returning to Presence

The first step is simply *noticing*. Noticing your surroundings. Noticing your own internal landscape. Noticing how often you are lost in thought—caught in the pull of the past or the worries of the future—and gently bringing yourself back to the present moment.

Without presence, everything else in this book remains an idea rather than an experience. Mindfulness begins with the ability to *be here*. To step outside of the mind's constant chatter and into full awareness of your breath, your body, the sensations around you. The rustling leaves, the feeling of the wind on your skin, the stillness between sounds. When you practice presence, you are practicing the art of truly *living*— experiencing life fully as it unfolds.

"Moves lightly, yet rests with absolute stillness."

Chapter 2. Breathing with the Earth

Once you have cultivated awareness, the next step is to *anchor* it. The breath is the bridge between mind and body, between thought and sensation. When you become aware of your breath you connect with the present moment in a deeper way.

Breath awareness is more than just a calming technique; it is a way of grounding yourself in your own being. It reminds you that you are alive, that you are here, that you are part of the greater rhythm of nature. Just as the trees breathe, just as the waves rise and fall, so too does your breath. It moves in a quiet, steady flow—always available to bring you back to yourself. By practicing breath awareness you create a foundation of steadiness and inner peace. No matter what happens, no matter where you are, your breath is always with you ready to guide you home.

Chapter 3. Open Your Heart to the Wild

With awareness and breath as your foundation, you can begin to move through the world with a more open heart. Mindfulness is not just about noticing—it is about *how* you choose to respond to what you notice.

When you connect with your heart you begin to live with greater patience, kindness, and forgiveness—not just for others, but for yourself. The more time you spend in nature, the more you see that everything is part of a cycle. The trees do not rush to grow. The seasons do not resist change. The river does not hold onto the past. When you bring this same gentle awareness to your own heart, you begin to soften. You begin to trust in life's unfolding.

This heart-centred approach to living shapes how you interact with yourself, with others, and with the earth. It allows you to move through the world with a sense of care—care for your own well-being, for those around you and for the land beneath your feet.

Let These Core Practices Settle Within You

These first three chapters are the foundation of all that follows. If you move through them too quickly, the rest of the journey will not feel as rich or meaningful. But if you take your time—if you allow awareness, breath and heart to become steady within you—then the practices ahead will unfold in a different way.

So take your time. Return to these practices again and again. Let them root deeply within you. And when you feel ready, allow them to guide you forward—into the wild, into stillness, into a life lived with deeper connection and care.

The next chapters invite you to create, explore, and express yourself in nature, but the depth of your experience will depend on how well you have embodied these core foundational skills. When presence is natural, when breath is steady, when your heart is open—you will not just *do* the practices, you will *feel* them, live them, and carry their essence with you far beyond these pages.

"The trees do not rush to grow."

Chapter 4: Awaken Your Senses

Have you ever noticed how a certain scent can bring back a vivid memory? How the sound of rain falling can make you feel instantly calmer? Our senses are powerful—they are our most direct way of experiencing the world. Yet, so often we move through life without truly engaging with them.

In nature our senses have the power to anchor us deeply in the present moment. This chapter invites you to expand your awareness beyond sight—to listen, touch, taste, and smell with curiosity. To feel the roughness of bark beneath your fingertips, to hear the subtle differences between wind through pine needles and wind through dry grass, to inhale the deep, earthy scent of damp soil after rain. When we awaken our senses the world becomes richer. We experience nature not just as a backdrop, but as something we are intimately connected to.

Chapter 5: Create with the Land

There is a natural creativity that emerges when we spend time in nature—not through effort, but through play. A child instinctively picks up a stick and draws in the dirt, arranges fallen leaves into patterns, or stacks stones into towers. This chapter invites you to return to that kind of expression, to create not for an outcome, but for the joy of creating.

Art, movement, and play are all ways of forming a relationship with the land. When we use natural materials—mud, sand, water, leaves, shadows—we are not separate from nature but interacting with it, responding to it. This chapter offers simple expressive ways to create *with* the land rather than *taking from* it, honouring nature's impermanence and beauty in the process. You don't have to be an artist. You just have to be willing to explore.

"You just have to be willing to explore."

Chapter 6: Storytelling with Nature

Nature is full of stories. The lines in a fallen leaf, the weathered rings of an ancient tree, the patterns left behind in the sand after a tide retreats—each carries a history, a whisper of something larger than itself. And we too, are part of this ongoing story.

This chapter invites you to explore storytelling as a way of deepening your relationship with the land. Through art, reflection and imagination, you will weave your own stories—ones inspired by the patterns, forms, and symbols found in nature. You may find yourself writing poetry based on the movement of water, creating leaf collages that represent your own inner landscape, or listening deeply to the wind as if it has a message just for you. Storytelling is how we make meaning. It is how we process emotions, experiences, and the lessons that nature has to teach us.

Chapter 7: Leaving No Trace (Ephemeral & Eco-Art)

Art is often thought of as something permanent—a painting framed on a wall, a sculpture meant to last for generations. But in nature everything is impermanent. The river carves new paths, the wind reshapes the dunes, the petals of a flower bloom and fall. What if we created *with* this impermanence?

This chapter explores the practice of ephemeral art—creating beauty that is meant to disappear. Arranging leaves into patterns only to let the wind carry them away, tracing designs in the sand knowing the tide will soon erase them, stacking stones that may tumble with the next breeze. These simple, mindful acts invite us to engage with nature without harming it, to create not for possession but for the joy of the process itself.

Chapter 8: Sacred Nature, Sacred Self

For thousands of years, people across cultures and traditions have seen nature as sacred—not as something separate from the divine, but as an embodiment of it. Many Indigenous cultures see the land as a teacher, a source of wisdom. In Hindu traditions, the elements—earth, water, fire, air—are not just physical forces but energies that exist within us all.

This chapter explores the deep connection between nature and the sacred, inviting you to experience the land not just as scenery, but as something alive and deeply interconnected with your own being.

"Energies that exist within us all."

Chapter 9: Giving Back to the Earth

Love, when deeply felt, cannot help but overflow. When we spend time in nature—truly seeing it, feeling it, breathing with it—something shifts within us. We stop thinking of the earth as something we use and start seeing it as something we *care for*. Giving back is not about obligation or guilt, it is about gratitude.

This final chapter brings the journey full circle, inviting you to turn your connection with nature into action. Giving back can take many forms. The scale does not matter. What matters is the intention—the choice to care, to nurture, to leave the earth a little better than we found it.

Chapter 10: Your Wild Stillness Journey

This final chapter is about integration. It offers gentle guidance on how to make time for your well-being, how to keep your connection with nature alive, and how to weave small but meaningful practices into everyday life. You will find simple actions and reflections in this chapter to help you stay rooted in presence and connection. A mindful breath taken beneath the sky. A pause to listen to the wind. A moment of gratitude for the earth beneath your feet.

"How to weave small but meaningful practices into everyday life."

The Practice Pages

Each chapter in *Wild Stillness* includes a series of practices designed to be an invitation—an opportunity to step into mindfulness, creativity, and connection with nature in a way that feels personal to you. The practice pages are structured to guide you through the experience, but they are not meant to be rigid instructions. Think of them as gentle signposts rather than rules to follow.

Each practice page includes:

Overview: A short introduction to the practice, what it involves, and the essence of what you are exploring.

Outcomes: The deeper benefits of the practice—how it supports mindfulness, creativity, presence, or connection with nature.

Items: A simple list of materials (if any) that may be helpful, most of which can be found in nature or at home.

Intention: A short guiding statement to help focus your attention and energy as you begin the practice. You can use the suggested intention or set your own.

Steps: A step-by-step guide to lead you into the practice, helping you engage fully in the experience.

Reflection: Thoughtful questions or prompts to help you deepen your awareness and integrate what you've experienced.

More: Additional ways to expand or adapt the practice, allowing you to explore it in different ways.

"Trust your intuition"

Making the Practice Your Own

Before you begin a practice, take a moment to *read through the page and the steps first* so you have a sense of what's ahead. This will help you enter the experience without needing to stop and refer back too often. However, once you begin, let go of any need to *follow exactly*. If another variation naturally unfolds as you practice—if your attention is drawn to something unexpected, if a new way of engaging with the activity arises—go with it. This journey is meant for *you*, and your experience will be unique.

There is no right or wrong way to practice, only what feels aligned in the moment. Trust your intuition. Let the practice evolve with you. Some days, it may feel quiet and still; other times, it may feel playful and expansive. Whatever arises, know that you are exactly where you need to be.

The Power of Setting Intentions

Before beginning any practice, taking a moment to set an intention can deepen your experience. Intentions are not rigid goals or expectations; they are gentle guiding lights helping to bring clarity and focus to what you hope to cultivate in your time with nature. They invite you to be present, to tune into your own needs, and to align your attention with what feels most meaningful to you in that moment.

Setting an intention can be as simple as choosing a word—peace, connection, stillness, gratitude—or a short phrase such as "I open myself to the wisdom of the land" or "I allow my breath to guide me into presence." Each practice in this book includes a suggested intention, but you are always welcome to choose one that resonates more deeply with your heart that day.

How to Set an Intention

1. **Bring your attention to the present.** Before beginning, pause for a moment. Acknowledge that this is a time for connection—with yourself, with nature, and with the present moment.
2. **Take a few deep breaths.** Inhale slowly, feeling the air move through your body. Exhale fully, letting go of any tension or distractions.
3. **Feel into your heart.** What do you need in this moment? What quality do you want to cultivate—peace, awareness, openness, joy? Trust whatever comes to you.
4. **State your intention.** Either silently or aloud, speak your intention: *"I invite stillness into this moment,"* or *"I offer my presence fully to the land."*
5. **Give gratitude.** Acknowledge this time as a gift—to yourself, to the earth, to the unfolding journey ahead.
6. **Begin your practice.** Carry your intention with you allowing it to subtly shape your awareness and deepen your experience.

Keeping a Journal or Collection

Throughout this journey, you might notice things shifting—your awareness, your breath, the way you experience the world around you. Keeping a small journal can help you reflect on these moments, capturing insights, sensations, or feelings as they arise.

You might also collect small natural objects—fallen leaves, shells, stones—to hold onto as reminders of your experiences. These small tokens can serve as anchors, bringing you back to a moment of stillness whenever you need it.

A Moment of Reflection

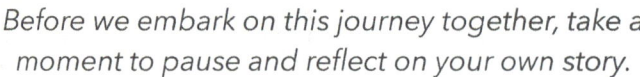

Before we embark on this journey together, take a moment to pause and reflect on your own story.

How has your relationship with nature shaped who you are? What is the strongest connection you feel with the natural world today?

_____
_____
_____
_____
_____
_____
_____

What do you hope to gain through this journey of wild stillness?

_____
_____
_____
_____
_____
_____

Allow these questions to gently guide your thoughts opening a space for honest reflection as you prepare to explore the path ahead. Your journey with nature—and with yourself—is unique and deeply meaningful.

Take this time to acknowledge it, for it is the foundation of all the discoveries to come.

Chapter 1:
Returning to Presence

The wind does not wonder where it has been,
nor the river where it flows next.
The tree does not rush to bloom,
nor does the bird regret yesterday's song.

But we—
we fill the space between moments with thoughts,
with lists and plans,
with echoes of the past and whispers of the future.

Yet stillness is waiting.
It hums in the hush of dawn,
in the pause between waves,
in the breath that rises and falls within you.

Presence – The First Step in the Journey

Being lost in our mind—caught in loops of thought, worry, planning, or replaying the past—is something many of us do without even realising. It becomes the background hum of our days. But over time, this mental busyness can take a real toll on our wellbeing. When we live from the neck up, disconnected from our body and surroundings, we may feel anxious, scattered, overwhelmed, or exhausted. Our nervous system stays on high alert, stress builds, and we miss the beauty of what's actually happening right now. We may feel like we're always behind, not enough, or disconnected from joy, even when nothing is "wrong." Being lost in the mind creates distance—from the world, from our own intuition, and from the quiet nourishment of simply being.

Presence is the gentle medicine that brings us home. It's paying attention to what is around you: the way sunlight filters through shifting leaves or the intricate details in a butterfly's wing. It's stepping out of the constant hum of your mind and into direct experience, where nature is not just something you observe but something you are a part of. But presence is more than just noticing the world outside of you. It is also turning that same awareness inward—paying attention to how you feel, how your body moves and responds, how your energy shifts in different landscapes. True presence is a meeting point between the external and the internal, between nature and self. And like anything worthwhile, it starts small and deepens over time. There is no finish line, no final mastery—just a lifelong unfolding.

When we shift our attention from our thoughts to the sensations in our body, the breath, or the natural world around us, something softens. We come out of the whirlwind of thinking and into the experience of life. Presence grounds us. It slows the racing mind. It reminds us that we are safe, that this moment is enough, and that peace is not somewhere far away—it's available here, now, in the sound of a birdcall, the feel of sunlight, or the rise and fall of breath. Presence reconnects us with the truth of the moment. And from that place, we can respond to life with more clarity, calm, and compassion—rather than reacting from fear, stress, or autopilot. It's not about stopping thoughts—it's about not being ruled by them. It's about returning, again and again, to this moment, this breath, this connection with the living world.

Insights from Ancient Wisdom on Presence

Across cultures and traditions, the practice of presence—being fully engaged in the moment—has been revered as a path to wisdom, harmony, and connection. Nature itself has long been a teacher of this way of being. In the natural world, every living being operates in the present moment. Trees do not rush to grow, animals move, rest, and hunt based on instinct and immediate awareness, fully engaged in the surroundings. Many Indigenous traditions around the world emphasise the wisdom of listening deeply to the land. In Australian Aboriginal culture, the concept of *Dadirri* (deep listening) teaches that true understanding comes not from rushing to respond, but from being still, quiet, and open to the voices of the earth and ancestors.

In many spiritual traditions, mindfulness and presence have been central to personal transformation. In Zen Buddhism, the practice of *shikantaza* (just sitting) teaches that enlightenment is not something to chase—it arises when we are fully present with what is.

Whether through the quiet wisdom of a forest or the insights of ancient seekers, the message remains the same: presence is the gateway to deep connection—with ourselves, with others, and with the living world around us.

The Challenge of Presence & Why It Takes Practice

Presence sounds simple—just *be here now*—but anyone who has tried knows that it's not always easy. Our minds are busy places, constantly planning, analysing, remembering, and reacting. We are often pulled into the past or projected into the future without even realising it. And while our body might be in nature, our attention is often somewhere else entirely.

This is not a personal failure—it's simply how the human mind works. In fact, being distracted is normal. We've spent most of our lives practising *not* being present, so of course it takes time and gentle effort to re-train the mind toward awareness. This is why presence is called a practice—because we return to it again and again, each time strengthening the 'muscle' of awareness.

When you notice that you've become distracted—during a practice, or even just in everyday life—this *is* the moment of practice. That noticing is powerful. It's a signal that you're waking up, returning to the present moment. What you choose to do next is where your growth lies.

Strategies to Support Presence

- **Gently return to your anchor** - Whether it's your breath, the feeling of your feet on the earth, the sound of birds, or the texture of bark beneath your fingers—use your senses as a bridge back into now.

- **Don't judge yourself** - The mind will wander. That's okay. What matters is how you respond. Meet the moment with kindness and curiosity, not frustration or self-criticism.

- **Take a slow breath** - A single mindful breath can shift your awareness in an instant. It grounds the body and quiets the mind.

- **Name what's happening** - Sometimes gently saying, *"thinking"* or *"worrying"* in your mind can help break the spell and bring you back.

- **Pause and feel** - If you've become caught in your head, stop for a moment. Tune into your body. Notice what you're feeling—physically or emotionally—and let yourself simply *be* with it.

- **Return with gratitude** - Every time you come back to presence, no matter how many times you've wandered, thank yourself. This is the journey.

Remember, presence isn't about holding your attention perfectly. It's about returning, again and again—with patience, kindness, and trust. Over time, the space between distraction and awareness grows shorter. You begin to live more moments *in* the moment—not only during nature practices, but in the everyday movements of your life. And this is where real change begins.

The following pages invite you to deepen your connection with *being* in nature, aware of your surroundings - and yourself.

"Alert yet calm, always listening to the moment."

Stillness Sit

Reconnect with your inner self through the quiet power of stillness. In this practice you find a quiet spot outdoors and simply sit, allowing yourself to be fully present. Create space to reconnect with your inner self and embrace the stillness within.

 **Outcomes**
- Cultivates mindfulness by encouraging you to be fully present.
- Fosters a deeper reconnection with your inner self through silence and observation.

 **Items**
A quiet outdoor space
A comfortable spot to sit (a bench, a rock, or patch of grass)

Intention: "I sit in stillness and allow my thoughts to pass without judgement."

 **Steps**

Find a peaceful outdoor spot that feels welcoming— maybe on a bench, a rock, or directly on the earth. Let your body settle into a relaxed posture, allowing yourself to feel supported by the ground beneath you. Close your eyes or simply lower your gaze. Begin by taking a few slow, deep breaths—just to arrive fully in this moment.

Let your awareness drop down into your body. Feel where you're touching the earth—the weight of your legs, the contact of your hands, the air brushing your skin. Notice the space around you. The sounds, the scent, the gentle presence of nature holding you.

There's nothing to fix or change. Nothing to achieve. Just be here, as you are.

Thoughts may come and go. That's natural. When they do, see if you can notice them without holding on—like clouds drifting across a quiet sky. Gently bring your attention back to your breath, your body, and the support of the earth beneath you.

Stay with this stillness for as long as feels right. Let this be a time of simply being, of softening into presence, of remembering your place in the great rhythm of the land.

 **Reflect**
How did it feel to just sit in stillness?
In what ways did this practice help you reconnect with your inner self?

 **More**
Experiment with this practice in different natural settings or at various times of the day to see how your experience of stillness changes.

Rooted Feet

Stand barefoot on the earth noticing sensations in your feet and the connection to the ground. This practice helps cultivate a sense of presence by focusing on the direct connection between the body and the earth.

 **Outcomes**
- Encourages awareness and grounding through direct contact with nature.
- Develops mindfulness by focusing on physical contact.

 **Items**
A safe outdoor space with grass, soil, sand, or another natural surface

Intention: "I ground myself in the present, feeling the earth's steady support beneath me."

 **Steps**

Find a place where you can stand barefoot on the earth. It might be soft grass, warm sand, or even a patch of forest floor. Let your feet settle about shoulder-width apart and take a moment to simply arrive. Lower your gaze or gently close your eyes. Begin by taking a few slow, deep breaths. Feel the rise and fall of your chest. Feel your body being breathed.

Now bring your awareness to your legs and feet. Notice the quiet strength of your stance. Feel your weight gently pressing down into the earth. Let your attention rest on the soles of your feet—the temperature of the ground, its texture, the contact where skin meets soil. There's no rush. Just feel.

Stand here for a little while, allowing stillness to rise. Imagine your body growing heavier, not in a burdensome way, but in a grounded, rooted way—like a tree standing tall in still air. If it feels right, begin to shift your weight slowly from one foot to the other. Notice how the muscles in your legs respond. Feel the earth supporting you with each gentle sway. Then come back to centre, letting your body find balance once more.

Now, with your next breath out, imagine roots growing from the soles of your feet—down through the soil, winding around stones, stretching deep into the earth. Each exhale sends them further. Each inhale draws steadiness back up into your body. Breathe out and root. Breathe in and receive.

 **Reflect**
What did you notice about feeling the ground beneath your feet? Did you feel more present and connected to nature?

 **More**
Try this practice on different natural surfaces (sand, grass, mud, smooth stones) and compare the sensations.

Panoramic Presence

Take in the vastness of the landscape—let your attention return to the now. In this practice, choose a sweeping view and slowly take in the entire landscape. As you gaze across the expanse, allow the vastness to pull you into the present moment.

 *Outcomes*
- Cultivates mindfulness by drawing your attention to the present moment.
- Fosters a deeper awareness of your body and how it feels in a vast space.

 *Items*
A location with a wide, sweeping view (hillside, valley, open field, etc.)

Intention: "I open myself fully to the expansive beauty around me."

 *Steps*

Find a spot in nature where you can see far—perhaps on a hill, a clifftop, or a wide open field. Stand or sit in a way that feels steady and relaxed, with your body open to the view ahead of you.

Take a few slow, grounding breaths. Let your shoulders soften. Allow your gaze to wander gently across the landscape—left to right, near to far—without needing to focus on any one thing. Just notice the whole scene unfolding before you.

Begin to observe the layers of the land. Can you see texture in the trees? Shadows cast by clouds? The soft rise and fall of the terrain? Look for movement—the sway of grasses, the drifting of birds, the play of light across surfaces. Let your eyes take it all in like a slow, spacious sweep. As you do, notice how your body responds to the openness. Perhaps there's a softening in your chest, or a quieting in your mind. Let the vastness of the view create a sense of inner spaciousness too. You might even feel your breath deepen naturally as you absorb the expanse before you.

If your mind drifts to thoughts or distractions, that's okay. Just gently bring your attention back to the land, to the sky, to the stillness that holds it all. Stay for as long as you like. Let this practice be a reminder that the world is wide, and that there's always room to pause, to breathe, and to be present in the middle of it all.

Reflect
How did the expansive view affect your sense of presence? Did the vastness help you feel more connected to the present?

 *More*
Try incorporating gentle movement into this practice by slowly walking along the edge of the view.

Water Reflection

Sit by a still pond or gentle stream and watch the surface. Allow the ripples to remind you of the ever-changing yet constant flow of the present moment. As you observe the ripples, reflect on the constant flow of life.

- Develops mindfulness by focusing your attention on the subtle movement of water.
- Encourages an appreciation for the continuous nature of the present.

A still pond, lake, or gentle stream
A comfortable spot to sit

Intention: "I allow the gentle flow of water to sooth my mind and renew my spirit."

Find your way to a quiet spot beside a still body of water—a gentle stream, a pond, or a calm corner of a lake. Settle into a comfortable seat where you can rest and feel held by the natural space around you. Let your body relax, and take a few deep, steady breaths to arrive fully.

Turn your attention toward the water. Let your gaze soften as you observe the surface. You might notice delicate ripples, gentle movements, or light dancing across it. Watch how the water shifts and flows, always in motion yet deeply calm.

As you sit, begin to see the water not just with your eyes but with your awareness. Notice how it mirrors the sky, the trees, and perhaps even your own inner state. Allow its fluidity to become your guide—a reflection of how you, too, are always shifting, always becoming.

If thoughts arise, greet them kindly and let them pass, like ripples gliding outward and fading away. You don't need to follow them. Just come back to the water, to its rhythm, to this moment.

Let yourself be fully here. There is nowhere else to be. Sit for as long as you wish, breathing with the land and the water, letting stillness rise within you like a reflection—quiet, steady, and alive.

How did watching the water affect your sense of time and presence? What did you notice about the movement and change in the water?

Try a gentle mindful walk along the water's edge, noticing how the flow of water mirrors the flow of your breath.

A Closer Look

Choose an interesting natural object that speaks to you. Spend time really exploring how it looks. What feelings or memories does it stir? As you observe closely, allow the object to evoke memories or feelings, creating a deeper connection with nature.

- Deepens sensory awareness through detailed observation.
- Fosters emotional insight by connecting visual details to personal feelings.

A natural object that catches your attention (a unique leaf, interesting stone, patterned flower, or piece of bark)

Intention: "I slow down and notice the tiny details of the world around me, opening my eyes to wonder"

As you wander outdoors, let your attention rest on a single natural object that quietly calls to you. It might be a weathered leaf, a twisted branch, a seedpod, a shell, or even a small stone. There's no need to search—just let something catch your eye or speak to your senses. When you've found it, gently gather it (if appropriate), and find a peaceful place to sit.

Take a few deep, steady breaths to arrive in this moment. Let the pace of your body slow, and place your full awareness on this small piece of the natural world.

Begin to explore the object with curiosity and care. Notice the colour—are there subtle shifts, speckles, patterns? Feel the texture beneath your fingers. Is it rough, smooth, delicate, firm? Examine the edges, the curves, the imperfections. You might turn it over in your hand or hold it up to the light, noticing how it changes from different angles.

Now go deeper. What feelings does this object stir in you? Does it remind you of a particular memory, a place, or a time in your life? Let your thoughts meander gently, allowing this object to be both anchor and mirror.

There's no need to rush. Let the act of noticing become a meditation—a quiet dialogue between you and this small piece of nature.

What memories or feelings arose as you examined the object?
How has this focused observation changed your perception of the object?

Capture the object's essence by sketching, photographing, or writing about it.

Birdwatching Presence

Find a quiet spot in nature and allow the beauty and energy of birds to anchor you in the present moment. Observe every detail allowing each moment to deepen your appreciation for the natural world.

 *Outcomes*
- Enhances sensory awareness and mindfulness by attuning you to the subtle details of nature.
- Encourages an appreciation for the joy and beauty found in the natural environment.

 *Items*
A quiet outdoor setting where birds are present (such as a park, garden, or forest clearing

Intention: "I listen to the voices of the birds, letting their songs draw me into awareness."

 *Steps*

Find a quiet place in nature where birds are active—perhaps a garden, field, or forest edge. Choose a spot where you can sit or stand undisturbed, and allow yourself to settle in gently. Take a few slow, grounding breaths. Feel your body relax and your senses begin to open. With each exhale, let go of anything that might pull you away from this moment.

Soften your gaze and begin to observe. Let your eyes wander slowly across the landscape. You might notice birds perched in trees, gliding across the sky or resting quietly nearby. Watch without expectation—simply allow yourself to witness.

Take in the details: the colours and patterns in their feathers, the way they move, the tilt of a head, the flick of a wing. Listen closely to their calls and songs. Each one a voice of the land. Let your awareness sink into the rhythm of their world. Feel their energy—alert, light, present.

If your mind wanders, just notice it, and gently bring your attention back to the birds.

Remain here for as long as you like, immersed in the gentle dance of birds and breeze. There is nothing to do but observe, breathe, and be part of this moment with them. When it feels time to leave, carry a little of that lightness with you.

 *Reflect*
How did observing the birds affect your sense of presence? Did it influence your mood or perspective?

 *More*
Try this practice at different times of day to observe how the birds and the overall ambience change .

Tree Connection

Lean against a sturdy tree and feel its enduring presence. Let the tree's calm energy invite you to reflect on your own inner stability. As you feel the tree's strong presence, allow it to remind you of your own inner stability and strength.

 *Outcomes*
- Develops a sense of groundedness and inner stability.
- Encourages mindful reflection on personal strength and resilience.

 *Items*
A sturdy tree in a quiet outdoor space.

Intention: "I connect with the enduring energy of the tree, drawing strength from its ancient presence."

 *Steps*

Find your way to a tree that feels strong and steady—one that draws you in with its quiet presence. Let yourself be guided by feeling. When you find the right one, come close.

Stand or sit beside the trunk and lean into it gently. Notice its texture beneath your fingers—rough or smooth, cool or warm from the sun. This tree has stood here through seasons and storms, rooted deeply in the earth, stretching quietly toward the sky.

Close your eyes, or let your gaze soften. Take a few deep, unhurried breaths. Feel your body begin to slow down. Let the tree support you—not just physically, but energetically. As you breathe, imagine its strength flowing into you. Feel its rootedness mirrored in your legs, its stillness echoing in your chest.

You don't need to do anything. Just be here, with the tree. Let its calm presence become your own. If your mind starts to wander, gently bring your attention back to the sensation of leaning, resting, breathing. Stay in this quiet connection for as long as you like. Let the tree remind you of your own stability, your inner strength, your place in the living world.

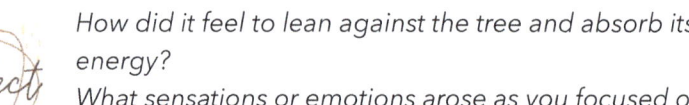 *Reflect*

How did it feel to lean against the tree and absorb its energy?
What sensations or emotions arose as you focused on the tree's support?

 *More*

Try pairing this practice with a walking meditation, slowly circling the tree and observing its details while reflecting on your inner strength.

Evening Contemplate

As dusk falls sit quietly under the emerging stars. As you watch the sky transition from day to night, reflect on your place in the universe and observe how this natural shift mirrors your inner journey.

- Enhances mindfulness by inviting you to slow down and observe natural transitions.
- Encourages introspection about your personal journey and place in the world.

A quiet outdoor space with a clear view of the sky

Intention: "I reflect on my day, allowing the fading light to transform my experiences into wisdom."

As the day begins to fade, find a quiet place where you can watch the horizon. Settle into a comfortable position, and allow the slowing rhythm of dusk to meet you.

Take several deep, steady breaths to land in the moment. With each exhale, release the busyness of the day and let yourself arrive—right here, right now.

As the light begins to change, turn your attention to the sky. Watch how the colours shift—soft gold, blush pink, fading blue. Notice how, without effort, the day hands itself over to the night. There is no resistance here, only a graceful unfolding. Let this be your guide.

As darkness deepens and stars begin to appear, observe how the whole landscape seems to settle. You might notice a hush in the air, a stillness settling in the trees. Let it all in.

This transition—from day to night—is nature's way of reminding you how to soften, to allow change, to let go. Notice any feelings that arise, or insights that flicker across your awareness. You don't need to chase them. Just watch and receive. Stay here as long as you wish, letting the sky's quiet transformation mirror your own.

How did watching the transition from day to night affect your sense of self?
What thoughts or emotions arose as you observed the emerging stars?

Try pairing this practice with gentle music.

Seasonal Change

Visit a familiar spot throughout the year and note subtle changes in the landscape. Reflect on the impermanence of nature and how it parallels your own inner evolution. This ongoing process helps you embrace change and find beauty in life's natural cycles.

 *Outcomes*
- Deepens mindfulness by encouraging you to observe change over time.
- Enhances your understanding of impermanence and personal growth.

 *Items*
A familiar natural location that you can revisit throughout the year.

Intention: "I embrace the shifting rhythms of nature, allowing myself to flow with change."

 *Steps*

Choose a natural place that feels meaningful to you—somewhere you can visit again and again throughout the year. It might be a quiet trail, a favourite tree, a garden, or a lookout point.

When you arrive take a few deep grounding breaths. Let your body settle into the landscape, and allow your attention to stretch gently outward. This is a practice of noticing—of arriving fully and being open to what this particular moment in the season wants to show you.

Begin to observe the details around you. What colours are present today? What is blooming, shedding, growing, or fading? Look closely—at the light, the textures, the shapes and shadows. Notice the way the air feels on your skin, the sounds around you, and how the earth holds itself in this season.

Reflect on your previous visit here. What has changed? What remains steady? Allow yourself to respond to the landscape—what draws your eye, what stirs something in you? Let this place become a mirror. Just as the landscape shifts with the seasons, so too do you. You grow, release, rest, and begin again. There's wisdom in these cycles, and being with them can gently remind you that change is not only natural—it's essential.

Stay for as long as you wish, then return again when the season changes.

 *Reflect*
What parallels can you draw between nature's cycles and your own inner evolution?
How did observing these changes influence your perspective on impermanence?

 *More*
Combine your observations with drawing, painting, or composing poetry inspired by each season.

Memory Walk

Take a slow walk through a favourite natural setting. As you move, recall a cherished memory and notice how the present moment deepens your connection to that feeling. This practice blends the warmth of your past with the richness of the here and now.

 *Outcomes*
- Deepens your ability to connect with both your past and present.
- Enhances mindfulness and sensory awareness through movement and reflection.

 *Items*
A natural setting that feels meaningful to you

Intention: "I invites memories to rise and settle, reminding me of my journey."

 *Steps*

Find a natural place that feels familiar and comforting—somewhere you can move slowly and freely. Let it be a place where your heart feels at ease.

Begin your walk slowly, taking your time to settle into the rhythm of your body and the land around you. Let your senses open—listen to the sounds that rise and fall around you, feel the textures beneath your feet, and notice the scents that drift through the air. There's no need to rush—this is not a walk to get anywhere, but a walk to feel more deeply.

As you move, gently bring to mind a cherished memory—something that brings a sense of warmth, joy, or tenderness. It might be from childhood, a recent moment with someone you love, or a time when you felt especially alive or peaceful.

Allow that memory to rise slowly. Let it blend with the sights and sounds of the present moment. How does the breeze, the birdsong, the scent of the earth deepen your connection to that memory? Let the feeling of it bloom again inside you.

Continue walking with this gentle rhythm—alternating your awareness between the present landscape and the memory you hold. Notice how one enhances the other, how the past and present can coexist, weaving together in a quiet act of presence.

As your walk comes to an end, pause. Stand still. Feel your feet on the earth.

 *Reflect*
How did recalling a cherished memory affect your experience of the walk?
What sensory details deepened your connection to that memory?

 *More*
Share your experience with a friend or loved one.

Mindful Pause

During your outdoor time, pause at intervals to silently ask yourself, "How am I here right now?" Let this question draw your awareness inward. Invite your attention to turn inward, deepening your connection with the present moment and with yourself.

- Develops mindfulness by encouraging self-reflection and present-moment awareness.
- Strengthens your ability to connect with your inner self during everyday outdoor moments.

A natural outdoor setting where you can pause comfortably

Intention: "I give myself permission to stop, breathe, and fully arrive in this moment."

As you move through the landscape take a moment to pause. Find a place to stop, whether seated on a rock, resting against a tree, or standing quietly with the earth beneath your feet.

Close your eyes if it feels comfortable, or let your gaze soften. Then, gently ask yourself, "How am I here right now?" Let the question echo within you—not as something to answer, but as something to feel.

Notice the sensations in your body—the rhythm of your breath, the placement of your feet, the openness or tension you might carry. Notice your thoughts too, and any emotions present. There is no need to change anything. Just witness.

Stay with this moment for as long as it feels natural, then slowly return to your movement.

When the impulse arises again—pause. Let your practice become a gentle rhythm of motion and stillness, each informing the other.

How did taking a mindful pause affect your sense of presence? What insights or feelings arose as you focused on the question "How am I here right now?"

Consider setting a gentle reminder or timer during your outdoor time to prompt regular mindful pauses.

Embodied Presence

Move your awareness from doing to being, feeling the rhythm of your body and the world around you. Feel each step, notice the textures beneath your feet, and absorb the sounds, smells, and sights of your surroundings. This practice invites you to hold your attention in the entire space, deepening your presence with every step.

 **Outcomes**
- Cultivates mindfulness by shifting your focus from habitual doing to being present.
- Enhances your connection with your body and the natural environment.

 **Items**

Anytime, anywhere

Intention: "I tune into my body's sensations, allowing them to guide me deeper into presence."

 **Steps**

Before you begin to walk, take a moment to stand still. Let yourself arrive. Feel your body in space and take several slow, deep breaths. When you feel ready, begin walking slowly. Pay close attention to the sensation of your feet meeting the ground. Notice the texture beneath you—is it soft, firm, uneven, cool? Feel how the earth holds you with every step.

Allow your body to find its own natural rhythm. Observe how you move—how your arms swing, how your weight shifts, how your breath accompanies your steps. Let this rhythm become a gentle anchor, drawing you deeper into presence.

Now begin to widen your awareness. What sounds are unfolding around you? What scents are drifting through the air? Let your eyes soften and take in the colours, light, and movement of the landscape. You are not just walking through nature—you are walking with it.

If your mind begins to wander, that's okay. Simply notice it with kindness, then guide your focus back to your body and the environment around you. The sensation of your foot lifting and landing. The warmth of the sun. The breeze on your skin. The steadiness of each moment.

Continue walking for as long as you like, letting each step be a practice in presence—a way of of remembering your body, your breath, and your belonging to the land.

 **Reflect**

Did shifting your focus from doing to being change your experience? Did attention in the entire space influence your sense of calm and connection?

 **More**

Include mindful pauses during your walk to fully absorb a specific element of your environment.

A Moment of Reflection

Before moving forward in your journey, take a moment to pause and reflect on your experience with presence.

What moments in nature have helped you feel truly present? Were there particular places, times of day, or natural elements that supported your awareness?

_____
_____
_____

What distractions pulled you away from presence? How did you respond when your mind wandered?

_____
_____
_____

How did your body feel when you were fully present? Did you notice any changes in tension, ease, or energy when you allowed yourself to be still and aware?

_____
_____
_____

Did your connection to nature feel different when you slowed down? How did the landscape, sounds, or sensations around you change when you were deeply present with them?

_____
_____
_____

Do you feel ready to move forward? The next chapter will explore breath—the bridge between body and earth.

There is no rush. Take your time, listen to what you need, and trust that each step is unfolding exactly as it should.

Chapter 2:
The Breath of the Earth

*The wind moves through the trees, whispering its ancient song.
The waves rise and fall, drawing the ocean's steady breath.
The earth itself exhales in mist and morning air, in the scent of rain, in the
warmth of the sun on your skin.*

*And you–
You breathe with it all.
With the forests and the rivers, the mountains and the sky.
With every inhale, you take in the world.
With every exhale, you give something back.*

*Breath is not just yours; it belongs to the earth, to the sky,
to the endless cycle of life moving through us all.*

*So breathe.
And remember–you are not separate.
You are part of this great, breathing world.*

From Presence to Breath

As we move into the practices of breath, we carry forward everything we have explored in the previous chapter on presence. The ability to be aware—to notice when your mind has wandered and gently return to the moment—is a skill you have already begun to develop. Just as presence allows us to fully engage with the world around us, it also strengthens our ability to turn inward, to observe the quiet rhythms of the body, and to connect with the breath as an anchor to the here and now.

The practices in this chapter build upon that foundation. They invite you to deepen your awareness—not just of your surroundings, but of the steady, life-giving flow of breath moving through you. As you engage with these exercises, you may find that your ability to stay with your breath, to witness its natural movement, and to return to it when the mind drifts, comes more easily. Like any practice, this awareness strengthens over time, becoming a steady and familiar presence in your daily life.

Close your eyes for a moment and take a slow, deep breath. Feel the air moving in, filling your lungs, expanding your chest. Then, let it go—softly, gently.

That breath you just took has been on a long journey. It has moved through forests, over oceans, across deserts. It has circled the globe, carried by winds, exhaled by trees, shaped by the rhythms of the earth itself.

The same air that rushes through your body also stirs the leaves, shapes the clouds, and carries the scent of rain. When we pause to notice it, to really feel it, we remember that we are not separate from nature—we are part of it.

Breath in Ancient Wisdom

Across cultures and traditions, breath has long been understood as more than just air moving in and out of the body—it is life force, spirit, and connection. Many ancient teachings recognise breath as a bridge between the self and the world, a thread that ties us to the rhythms of nature.

In Indigenous Australian wisdom, the land itself is alive and breathing. The concept of Songlines speaks to an intimate relationship between breath, sound, and the earth, where ancestral songs map the landscape and connect people to Country. Breathing in these sacred places is a way of listening—to the land, to the ancestors, to the wisdom carried in the wind.

In yogic traditions, breath is known as prana, the vital life force that flows through all living things. The way we breathe shapes our energy, our awareness, and our connection to the greater whole. By breathing deeply and with intention, we attune ourselves to the natural world and the unseen currents that sustain it.

In modern ecology, we now understand that trees and plants "breathe" alongside us, exchanging carbon dioxide and oxygen in a perfect, life-sustaining cycle. Forests, in a sense, inhale and exhale with us, making every breath a quiet collaboration between human and tree, sky and soil.

How Slow, Mindful Breathing Supports Body and Mind

Slow, mindful breathing is one of the simplest yet most powerful tools we have to support both our physical and mental well-being. When we slow the breath and bring conscious awareness to it, we create a ripple effect throughout the body—activating systems that calm, restore, and rebalance us.

Physiological Benefits

Mindful breathing directly influences the nervous system, especially the parasympathetic branch—often called the "rest and digest" system. This is the opposite of the stress-driven "fight or flight" response. When we breathe slowly and deeply, it signals to the body that we are safe, allowing the heart rate to slow, blood pressure to drop, and muscles to relax. Over time, this can reduce inflammation, improve digestion, support immune function, and help regulate hormones. Mindful breathing also increases oxygen flow throughout the body, helping your cells to function more efficiently. It helps regulate the vagus nerve, a key player in emotional regulation and resilience.

Mental and Emotional Benefits

Mentally, slow breathing helps quiet the mind. It reduces anxious thoughts and creates a sense of spaciousness between stimulus and response. Instead of reacting impulsively, we begin to respond with more calm and clarity. It enhances focus, presence, and our ability to regulate emotions—especially during times of stress or overwhelm. And emotionally, the breath becomes a gentle companion. It helps ground us in the moment and soothes the intensity of difficult feelings. In this way, mindful breathing can be both an anchor and a balm—helping us meet life with greater steadiness, patience, and ease.

Anchoring the Breath

At first, paying attention to your breath may seem simple. After all, you've been breathing your whole life without effort. Yet the moment you try to focus on it, distractions rush in—thoughts pull you elsewhere, sensations in the body call for attention, sounds in the environment tug at your awareness. This is natural.

The mind is wired to wander, constantly scanning for what's next, what was, what could be. It takes patience to meet this tendency with kindness instead of frustration. Returning to the breath is not about forcing stillness or achieving perfect focus. It's about noticing when you've drifted and gently bringing yourself back. Again and again.

One of the most powerful things about using the breath in mindfulness practice is its constant presence. Unlike other tools for awareness—like a journal, a meditation cushion, or time in nature—your breath is something you always have with you. You don't need to pack it in your bag, schedule time for it, or remind yourself to bring it along. It is simply there, moving through you in every moment, no matter where you are or what you're doing.

This makes breath an incredibly accessible anchor for mindfulness. Whether you are sitting in stillness, walking through a forest or waiting in line at the grocery store, you can always return to the breath. A single inhale, a single exhale—each one is an opportunity to step into presence.

Sunrise Breath

With each inhale, imagine welcoming light and warmth, and with each exhale, releasing the night. visualise drawing in the light, warmth, and energy of a new day. With each exhale, let go of the darkness and fatigue of the night.

- Enhances breath awareness and connects you with the natural cycle of renewal.
- Encourages the release of past tensions and the welcoming of positive energy.

A quiet outdoor space with a clear view of the sunrise

Intention: "As I inhale, I welcome new beginnings. As I exhale, I let go of what no longer serves me."

Rise early and make your way to a place where you can witness the day's first light. Let the moment be quiet and simple, just you and the light about to arrive. Sit comfortably, your spine tall and your shoulders soft. Feel the coolness of the morning air, the stillness before the world awakens. As the first golden hues begin to edge over the horizon, take a deep breath in through your nose. Imagine drawing the light into your body—filling yourself with the warmth, promise, and energy of a new day.

As you slowly exhale through your mouth, release anything that belongs to the night—tension, worry, heaviness. Let it flow out gently, carried away on the breath.

Continue this rhythmic breathing as the sky brightens. With each inhale, invite in light, hope, and clarity. With each exhale, soften into release. Feel your breath rise with the sun, steady and spacious.

Remain here for as long as you like, breathing with the rhythm of the dawn. When you're ready to move on, take one final deep inhale, hold it for a moment, and then exhale slowly.

How did the experience of inhaling light and exhaling darkness influence your mood?
What sensations did you notice in your body as you practised this breathing?

Observe how the emerging light and warmth influence your thoughts and feelings throughout the morning.

Breath of the Land

Tune into the breath of forests, rivers, and open skies through deep listening and presence with the natural world. Allow these natural sounds to guide you into a state of mindful presence as you connect with the living energy of the environment.

 *Outcomes*
- Develops deep listening skills and mindfulness by tuning into nature's rhythms.
- Enhances your connection with the environment through sensory awareness.

 *Items*
A quiet natural setting where you can hear a variety of sounds

Intention: "I breathe in the essence of the land around me, allowing nature's breath to become my own."

 *Steps*

Find a peaceful place in nature where you can sit comfortably. Choose a spot where the sounds of the natural world can reach you without distraction. Let your body relax into a gentle posture, upright but soft. You can close your eyes or keep them slightly open, whatever helps you feel most at ease. Take a few deep breaths, allowing your mind to slow and your senses to open.

Begin to listen—not just with your ears, but with your whole body. Tune in to the layers of sound around you: the rustling of leaves, the hum of insects, the rhythm of flowing water, the distant call of birds. Imagine the land itself is breathing—and that you are breathing with it.

There's no need to label or analyse. Simply receive. Let each sound arrive and pass like waves. Notice how your own breath begins to move in harmony with what you hear.

If thoughts arise, let them drift away like wind through grass. Gently return to the landscape's rhythm, to the breath of the earth as it moves through sound and silence alike.

Stay in this quiet listening for as long as you like. When you're ready, take one final deep breath, slowly open your eyes, and return to the day—carrying with you the quiet knowing that nature is always breathing with you.

 *Reflect*
How did listening to the land affect your sense of calm and presence? What sounds stood out to you, and how did they make you feel?

 *More*
Consider journaling about your experience or creating a visual representation of what 'breath of the land' means to you.

Tree Breathing

Breathe with the wisdom of the trees. This simple yet powerful practice helps you connect with nature's rhythm. By aligning your breath with a tree's presence, you cultivate awareness, grounding, and a sense of connection to the natural world.

 **Outcomes**
- Encourages mindful breathing and present-moment awareness.
- Fosters a sense of grounding and connection with nature.

 **Items**
A tree to stand beside
Barefoot optional for deeper connection

Intention: "I breathe deep into the earth and reach higher into possibility."

 **Steps**

Wander until you find a tree that gently calls your attention. It might be tall and towering or small and graceful—simply choose one that feels right in this moment. Approach slowly and stand beside it, or if it feels natural, rest your hand on its trunk.

Soften your gaze or close your eyes. Take a moment to notice the texture of the bark beneath your fingers, the scent of leaves or soil, the subtle sound of branches above. Feel the quiet strength of this tree—rooted, steady, alive.

Begin to breathe deeply. Inhale through your nose, imagining the breath drawing strength and energy up from the tree's roots, travelling into your body and anchoring you. With each exhale through your mouth, feel yourself gently sway—like branches moving in the breeze—releasing tension, letting go.

Let this rhythm continue for several minutes. Breathe in grounded stillness. Breathe out with ease and flow. The tree does not force anything—it simply stands, breathes, and belongs. Let it teach you. When you feel ready, open your eyes. Notice how your body feels now.

 **Reflect**
How did it feel to connect your breath with the movement of the tree?
What did you notice about your body's stability and balance?

 **More**
Try this practice with different trees and notice how each one makes you feel.

Wave Breathing

Let the rhythm of water guide your breath. Water is always in motion—flowing, rising, and falling in a natural rhythm. In this practice, you tune into the movement of waves, ripples, or even the gentle lapping of water to guide your breath.

 *Outcomes*
- Strengthens breath awareness and mindfulness.
- Promotes a sense of calm by syncing with nature's rhythm.

 *Items*
A body of water (ocean, lake, river, or even a small pond)

Intention: "I inhale and exhale with the rhythm of the waves, allowing my breath to flow like the tide."

 *Steps*

Find a quiet place beside a body of water—a beach, a riverbank, or a small lake where you can sit comfortably and feel at ease. Settle into your body and take a few slow, steady breaths. Let your body relax. Soften your gaze as you turn your attention toward the water. Watch its movement—whether it's the rise and fall of waves, the pulsing ripple of a stream, or the slow shift of tide against stone.

Begin to breathe with it. Inhale as the water rises or flows toward you. Exhale as it recedes or draws away. Let your breath follow this pattern—effortless and flowing. There's no right pace, just the natural rhythm of water and breath moving together.

Feel how your body begins to soften. Let tension slip away with each outward breath. Notice how being with the water slows your mind, how your awareness deepens as your breath becomes part of its rhythm.

After a few minutes, you might choose to gently close your eyes. Even without seeing the waves, imagine their movement—rising, falling, flowing, returning. Let your breath mirror this motion, staying connected to the pulse of the earth. When you feel ready, take one final deep inhale and a long, slow exhale.

 *Reflect*
How did it feel to connect your breath with water's movement? Did you notice any shifts in your thoughts or emotions?

 *More*
Try this practice with different bodies of water—waves at the ocean, ripples in a pond, or even rain falling.

Wind Breathing

Breathe with the wind, feeling its movement through you. The wind is constantly moving—flowing through trees, across open fields, and over water. In this practice, you connect with the wind's presence, allowing its movement to guide your breath.

- Deepens breath awareness by syncing with natural elements.
- Fosters connection with the wind as a force of change and renewal.

A breezy outdoor space

Intention: "I invite the wind to guide my breath, feeling its movement cleanse and refresh me."

Find a place where you can truly feel the wind—brushing your skin. Let yourself be still for a moment, standing with open awareness in this ever-moving, invisible presence.

Close your eyes or let your gaze soften. Notice how the wind dances around you. Does it swirl gently or rush in waves? Is it cool or warm? Let yourself be touched by it—welcomed by it.

Take a deep breath in, and imagine you're drawing in the wind itself—fresh, alive, full of energy. As you exhale, release fully—let the wind carry away whatever you're holding onto, like leaves falling from branches.

Continue to breathe this way—deep, slow inhales that fill you with clarity and movement, followed by soft exhales that surrender to the breeze. Let your breath begin to mirror the wind. If it picks up, let your breath be strong. If it softens, slow with it. Become part of the dance.

Let yourself be present in this shared rhythm—the wind and your breath moving together, free and uncontained. Feel the spaciousness it creates within you. When you feel complete, take one final deep inhale and a long exhale filled with gratitude—for the wind, for your breath, and for this quiet moment of connection with the wild air around you.

What did you notice about the wind's movement as you breathed with it? How did this practice make you feel—lighter, calmer, more connected?

Try Wind Breath in different places—on a windy hill, in a sheltered forest, or near the ocean.

Mountain Breathing

Breathe in strength. Breathe out steadiness. Mountains stand tall through every season, unmoved by storms and softened by sunlight. This practice invites you to embody the mountain's presence—strong, steady, and grounded.

- Cultivates a sense of stability and inner strength.
- Encourages connection with the stillness and resilience of nature.

A quiet outdoor space (near a mountain or open landscape if possible)

Intention: "I breathe with the strength and steadiness of the mountains."

Find a place where you can stand tall and undisturbed. Let your feet settle firmly into the earth, about hip-width apart. Feel the ground beneath you, solid and supportive. Begin to imagine your body as a mountain—strong, steady, unmoving.

Close your eyes or let your gaze soften. Let your arms rest naturally by your sides. Take a deep, slow breath in, and imagine the energy rising from your feet all the way to the crown of your head, filling you with quiet strength and spaciousness.

As you exhale, feel yourself grounding even more deeply—your body sinking into stillness, just like a mountain rooted in the land. Let your breath create this rhythm: inhaling to rise, exhaling to settle.

Stay with this breath, gently and naturally. If thoughts drift in, let them pass like clouds crossing a mountain sky—noticed, but not held. There is nothing to do but breathe and be.

Remain in this practice for a few minutes, standing strong, still, and present. When you feel ready to end, take one final deep inhale, and exhale with a sense of gratitude—for the mountain within you, and for the earth that holds you steady.

How did it feel to embody the presence of a mountain? What parts of your body felt most strong and grounded?

Try Mountain Breath in different weather conditions—on a calm day, in the wind, or with the sun warming your skin.

Moon Breathing

Under moonlight, breathe in cool, silvery air and exhale any heaviness, feeling lunar calm. Invite a sense of clarity and calm into your being, and let go of heaviness and tension, aligning your inner rhythm with the gentle, restorative pulse of the lunar night.

 *Outcomes*
- Enhances your ability to tune into natural rhythms and adjust your energy accordingly.
- Develops breath awareness for both energising and calming states.

 *Items*
A quiet outdoor space with a clear view of the moon

Intention: "I breathe in the soft, reflective energy of the moon, exhaling all that I am ready to release."

 *Steps*

Find a peaceful place outdoors where you can sit quietly beneath the night sky. Choose a spot where you can see the moon. Let its gentle presence draw you in. Sit comfortably. Let your hands rest loosely in your lap or on your knees. You might softly gaze at the moon, or close your eyes and simply feel its presence shining above you.

Begin by taking a slow, deep breath in through your nose, and imagine that you are drawing in the moon's silvery light—cool, calming, and serene. Feel it enter your body like a soft glow, washing through your chest and settling your mind.

As you exhale gently through your mouth, imagine letting go of any heaviness—any thoughts, tension, or emotions that no longer need to be carried. Let the night receive it all.

Continue this steady rhythm, breathing in the quiet light of the moon, and breathing out a sense of release. Let your breath move slowly, like the tide beneath moonlight—gentle, rhythmic, and full of grace. When you feel ready, let your breath return to its natural rhythm. Gently open your eyes if they were closed. Sit for a moment longer beneath the sky.

 *Reflect*
How did breathing under the moonlight influence your sense of calm and presence?
What sensations did you notice in your body as you inhaled the cool air and exhaled tension?

 *More*
Try a gentle moonlit walk, allowing the quiet energy of the night to deepen your connection with nature and your inner self.

Stillness
Between Breaths

Finding presence in the pause—the quiet space where stillness lives. Between every inhale and exhale, there is a brief moment of stillness—a space of quiet, presence, and possibility. This practice invites you to notice and rest in that pause.

 *Outcomes*
- Cultivates awareness of the quiet spaces within and around you.
- Strengthens the ability to sit in stillness without rushing to the next moment.

 *Items*
A quiet outdoor space (under a tree, by water, or anywhere peaceful)

Intention: "– I rest in the quiet space between inhale and exhale, embracing the deep stillness within me."

 *Steps*

Find a comfortable place in nature where you can sit or stand with ease—somewhere that feels spacious and calm. Let your body settle into the moment, and soften your gaze or gently close your eyes if that feels right.

Take a slow, steady breath in. At the top of that inhale, notice the brief, quiet pause—the stillness before the breath turns. Then exhale slowly, and observe the stillness again before your next inhale naturally begins. Let your awareness rest in these quiet in-between spaces.

Without trying to control your breath, simply allow it to flow—and begin to tune into the soft pauses between each inhale and exhale. As you breathe, widen your awareness to the landscape around you. Notice the stillness in the world too—the pause between birdcalls, the space between wind gusts, the gentle quiet when nothing is moving. Let your attention rest in these silences, like sinking into a calm pool of water.

If your thoughts begin to wander, gently guide them back—not with force, but with tenderness—to the pauses, the breath, the stillness. This is your anchor. Remain here for as long as it feels good. When you're ready, take a final deep breath, feel the spaciousness within you, and slowly return to your surroundings.

 *Reflect*

How did it feel to focus on the space between breaths?
What did you notice about your mind in the moments of stillness?

 *More*

Try bringing this awareness of stillness into other areas of your life—pausing before responding in conversation or rushing on.

Cyclic Breathing

Experience balance and calm through the flow of your breath and the natural energy around you. In this practise, you regulate your breath by alternating between your nostrils, creating a gentle rhythm that balances your mind and body.

 *Outcomes*
- ✦ Develops breath awareness and energy balance through a mindful connection with nature.
- ✦ Helps you connect with your inner self and the natural environment through breath regulation.

 *Items* A quiet outdoor space

Intention: "I restore balance within myself, harmonising my energy like the rhythms of nature."

 *Steps*

Find a peaceful outdoor spot. Settle into a comfortable seated position, letting your spine rise tall and your shoulders soften. Take a few natural breaths as you tune into the sounds, scents, and sensations around you. When you're ready, bring your right hand to your face and gently close your right nostril with your thumb. Breathe in slowly through your left nostril, imagining that you're drawing in fresh, clear energy from the land around you—air infused with trees, sky, and sunlight.

Pause for a brief moment. Then close your left nostril using your ring finger, release your thumb, and exhale slowly through your right nostril. As the breath leaves your body, visualise it carrying away any tension or heaviness, returning it to the earth with gratitude.

Now, breathe in through the right nostril, drawing in more of nature's calm and vitality. Close the right nostril with your thumb, release your ring finger, and exhale through the left nostril— letting go, softening, releasing.

Continue this gentle cycle of breath—left in, right out; right in, left out—moving slowly and with full awareness. Let your breath feel balanced, steady, and smooth, like a quiet rhythm echoing the harmony of the natural world. With each inhale, feel yourself becoming more refreshed and present. With each exhale, feel the earth receiving what you no longer need.

When you feel ready to finish, return your hand to your lap and allow your breathing to settle naturally.

 *Reflect*

How did nature enhance your experience of alternate nostril breathing? What sensations did you notice in your body as you visualised drawing in nature's energy?

More

Experiment with practising in different natural settings to observe how this influences your energy and mood.

Full Circle Breathing

There's something ancient and calming about turning in a slow, full circle—just as the earth turns, just as the seasons return again and again. In this practice, you'll stand in an open space and breathe as you turn, feeling yourself at the centre of the wide, wild world. As your body moves and your breath flows, you sense the quiet stillness that holds everything.

 **Outcomes**
- Develops breath awareness and the ability to shift with ease.
- Explore breath and body awareness while fostering a sense of wholeness, spaciousness, and belonging in the natural world.

 **Items**
An outdoor space with room to move

Intention: "I come home to myself at the centre of the circle."

 **Steps**

Step into an open space in nature. Let yourself pause here for a moment. Feel your feet connect with the earth beneath you, and sense the openness of the space around you. Take a few slow, steady breaths, letting your shoulders drop and your body relax. Allow yourself to arrive fully, knowing there's nowhere else you need to be.

When you feel ready, begin to slowly turn in place. Let your breath guide you—perhaps inhaling as you start your rotation, exhaling as you continue to move. There's no rush. Let the turning be gentle and deliberate, as if your breath is painting a circle in space.

As you move, open your awareness to everything around you. Notice the shifts in light, the colours that emerge from each direction, the sounds that greet you as you face a new part of the landscape. Let your breath expand with your view—reaching outward, touching the world with presence.

Eventually, you'll return to where you began. Come to stillness once more. Pause. Feel what it's like to come full circle—not just with your body, but with your breath, your awareness, and your connection to the earth. Let this stillness settle into you. Breathe, and be here.

 **Reflect**
What did you notice as you turned in a full circle? Did any particular direction or view catch your attention or feel different in your body?

 **More**
Try this practice at different times of day—dawn, midday, dusk.

Gifting Your Breath

Focus on your exhale, visualising it as a gift of positive energy and gratitude to the natural world. Focus on the outward exhale as a way to send warmth, gratitude, and healing energy into the environment. As you exhale, imagine your breath mingling with the air, connecting you with the natural world in a mindful, reciprocal exchange.

- Enhances breath awareness by encouraging you to focus on the outward flow of your exhale.
- Fosters a deeper connection with nature

A quiet outdoor space where you can sit or stand

Intention: "I offer my breath to the earth in gratitude."

Find a peaceful place in nature—a spot where you feel held by the land. Sit or stand comfortably, allowing your spine to lengthen and your shoulders to soften. Take a few slow, deep breaths, gently arriving in the present moment. Feel the earth beneath you, the air on your skin, the sounds that weave through the space around you.

Now begin to bring awareness to your exhale. With each breath out, imagine it as a gentle offering—a quiet gift from your body to the earth. Not forced or heavy, but soft and sincere. Let your breath carry your gratitude, your care, your presence. Let it be a way of saying: I am here, and I honour this place.. Know that your breath mingles with the breath of the trees, the breeze, the soil. It's all part of the same rhythm.

Continue for several minutes, simply breathing with intention. With every outward breath, give something kind and healing to the land that surrounds you. And with each inhale, receive its quiet support in return.

Stay with this gentle exchange as long as it feels right. When you're ready to move on, take one final breath—a quiet thank you—and carry the spirit of this offering with you.

How did visualising your outward breath as a gift to nature affect your experience?
What sensations or emotions arose as you focused on sending your breath outwards?

Integrate this practice into a daily routine or combine it with a mindful walk .

Wild Breath

Your breath and body are part of the living landscape—moving with the wind, stretching like the trees, flowing like water. Bring your awareness to how your breath and movement align with nature, deepening your sense of connection with the breath of the earth.

 *Outcomes*
- Encourages mindfulness by syncing breath with movement in nature.
- Cultivates a sense of flow, adaptability, and openness through movement.

 *Items*
An outdoor space where you can move freely.

Intention: "I breathe deeply, freely, wildly—honouring the untamed, natural essence of my being."

 *Steps*

Step outside and find a place where you have room to move—a trail, a field, a forest path, or even your own backyard. Let the air greet you. Stand still for a moment and simply breathe. Inhale deeply, noticing how the breath rises through your chest, how it fills you. Exhale slowly, letting the breath fall. Feel yourself soften into the rhythm of breath.

When you're ready, begin to walk. Let it be slow and mindful. With each step, match the rhythm of your breath—perhaps inhaling as one foot lifts and exhaling as it settles onto the earth. Let your breath guide your pace, your focus, your connection to the land beneath you.

Pause and stretch. Reach your arms up like the tall trees stretching toward the sky. Fold forward slowly, breathing deeply. Stand tall. Open your chest wide, arms outstretched, filling you lungs. Let each movement be an echo of the earth's rhythms in connection with your breath.

And then—move freely. Let your body respond to what you feel. You might sway, twist, rise, or spiral. There's no right way to move—just follow the rhythm of your breath and the feeling of being alive in this space. Move like a stream, like wind, like shadow and light. Be Wild!

When your movement feels complete, come back to stillness. Stand or sit, breathing gently. Feel the echo of your movement still vibrating in your body.

 *Reflect*
How did syncing breath and movement change your sense of presence in nature?
Which movements felt most natural or freeing?

 *More*
You might also pair this practice with music inspired by nature, letting the rhythm guide your flow.

A Moment of Reflection

Before stepping into the next chapter, take a moment to reflect on your journey with breath.

How did it feel to bring attention to your breath in nature? Did you notice any shifts in your energy, emotions, or state of mind?
_____
_____
_____

How did your breath change in different environments? Did breathing with trees, wind, or water feel different than breathing in stillness?
_____
_____
_____

What did you learn about the connection between breath and nature? Did you feel the way your inhale and exhale are part of the larger rhythm of the earth?
_____
_____
_____

How has awareness of your breath influenced your sense of presence? Do you find yourself pausing to notice your breath more throughout the day?
_____
_____

Do you feel ready to move into the heart? The next chapter invites you to explore emotions, love, and deeper connection. Does this feel like a natural next step, or would you like to spend more time with your breath?

Trust your pace. There is no rush. Each breath, each moment, is part of the unfolding journey.

Chapter 3:
Open Your Heart to the Wild

*In the quiet hush of dawn, let your heart unfold,
a tender bloom awakening to the call of the wild.
Embrace the untamed spirit of ancient trees,
the wind's soft murmur, the distant cry of freedom—
each note a reminder that life pulses boldly here.*

*Let your heart open like the vast, endless sky,
filled with the colour and chaos of nature's dance.
In every rustle of leaves and whisper of the breeze,
find a gentle invitation to release, to be
vulnerable and alive in the wild embrace.*

*Open your heart wide, and in its open space,
discover the untold magic of the wild within you.*

Open Your Heart to the Wild

You've already begun to lay a beautiful foundation—learning to return to the present moment through awareness, and gently anchoring that awareness with the rhythm of your breath. These practices are core to mindful living. They settle the mind, ground the body, and allow you to soften into stillness.

Now, from this place of steadiness, the journey continues—into the heart.

Presence and breath create the conditions for something deeper to unfold: the opening of your emotional self. The heart is where we begin to feel more fully—not just the beauty of nature around us, but the subtle stirrings within. It's the place where gratitude awakens, where compassion begins to bloom, and where we remember that we are not just observers of the natural world—we are part of it.

This chapter invites you to explore the wildness and tenderness of your own heart through simple, heartfelt practices in nature. As you slow down and begin to notice the colours of a sunset, the joy in birdsong, or the softness of a breeze against your skin, you may feel your heart begin to respond. That response—whether it comes as warmth, tears, a smile, or a sense of quiet awe—is the heart opening.

We often protect the heart without realising it, but in nature, something shifts. The land feels safe. The trees don't judge. The sky holds space for everything. Here, we can let ourselves feel again—softly, gently, at our own pace. And in doing so, we begin to remember the deep emotional wisdom that lives inside us: the capacity to love, to care, to forgive, and to feel joy.

This chapter is not about being emotional for the sake of it. It's about listening to the heart as another source of truth—just as vital as the mind and body. With presence and breath already with you, you now have what you need to move deeper. Let nature be your companion in this, and let your heart open, in its own wild, beautiful way.

Why Does This Matter? Why Open Our Hearts?

In a world that often values *doing* over *feeling*, and *thinking* over *being*, the heart can become a quiet, forgotten place. But it is here—in the gentle centre of your chest—that your deepest connections live. When you open your heart, you begin to see the world differently. Not through the lens of expectation or judgement, but through kindness, compassion, patience, and care. These are not abstract ideals; they are ways of being that bring richness, resilience, and meaning to your life.

When we open our hearts to the wild, we begin to live in right relationship—not only with the natural world, but with ourselves and each other. We become more attuned to the sacredness of life, more willing to pause, to care, to heal. An open heart allows joy to blossom, but also creates space for sorrow, for forgiveness, for the fullness of being human.

And in a world that desperately needs more kindness, more empathy, more reverence for the earth and all its beings—your open heart matters.

The Qualities of an Open Heart

Opening your heart is not just about feeling more—it is about *being more*. More present, more compassionate, more connected to the world around you. It is a way of moving through life with softness and strength, with tenderness and resilience. When we allow ourselves to fully feel, to embrace both joy and sorrow, we become more deeply human, more attuned to the quiet pulse of life that flows through all things.

An open heart is not fragile; it is vast. It does not close itself off for protection but expands in the face of life's experiences. It is through this openness that we cultivate the qualities that bring us, and the world, into greater harmony.

Compassion

Compassion is the ability to witness suffering—our own or another's—and respond with care instead of turning away. It is the gentle voice within that says, I see you. I understand. You are not alone. When we practice compassion, we recognise that all beings—humans, animals, trees, rivers—experience struggle, and that our kindness can ease that burden.

Love

Love is the foundation of an open heart. It is not just romantic or personal—it is the love that radiates outward to all things. It is the feeling of wonder when standing beneath a vast, star-filled sky. The deep appreciation for the intricate veins of a leaf. The quiet, overwhelming sense of connection that comes from walking barefoot on the earth.

Gratitude

Gratitude shifts our awareness from what is lacking to what is already here. It is the recognition of all that we have been given—the air in our lungs, the earth beneath our feet, the friendships and moments of joy that shape our lives.

Empathy

Empathy is the bridge between beings—it allows us to step into another's experience and feel as they feel. To hear the sorrow in someone's voice and feel it resonate in our own chest. To see an animal suffering and instinctively want to help. To witness a tree swaying in the wind and sense its quiet endurance.

Kindness

Kindness is love in action. It is the small, simple gestures that ripple outward—helping another without being asked, leaving an offering for the land, speaking gently to those who need warmth. A truly open heart does not hesitate to give because it understands that giving and receiving are the same.

Service

An open heart is not just about personal transformation; it is about how we show up for others—both human and non-human. When we open ourselves fully, we feel a responsibility to care, to nurture, to protect. We no longer see ourselves as separate from the earth, but as its caretakers.

Heart Connection with Nature in Ancient Wisdom and Traditions

Across cultures and traditions, the heart has been seen as more than just an organ—it is the centre of wisdom, intuition, and connection. Many ancient teachings recognise the deep relationship between the human heart and the natural world, seeing the earth itself as a living, breathing entity that speaks to us through its rhythms, cycles, and quiet presence.

Many Indigenous cultures view the land as a sacred, living being—one that is deeply intertwined with the human spirit. In Australian Aboriginal culture, the concept of *Country* goes beyond physical land; it is a spiritual presence, an ancestral force that holds stories, memories, and a deep sense of belonging. To walk on the land is to connect with the heart of the earth, and in doing so, we reconnect with our own hearts.

In Taoist philosophy, the human heart (*Xin*) is not just a place of emotion but a gateway to deep understanding. Taoism teaches that when we attune to nature's effortless flow—the way rivers move, the way seasons change—we bring our own hearts into balance. The more we align with the rhythms of the earth, the more we cultivate inner peace and emotional clarity.

In Buddhism, the heart is the centre of *metta*, or loving-kindness—a practice that extends beyond human relationships to include all beings. Many Buddhist teachings encourage sitting in nature, contemplating the interconnectedness of life, and opening the heart with compassion for both self and the world.

In Hindu philosophy, the heart is associated with the *Anahata* chakra—the energy centre linked to love, connection, and emotional healing. The Anahata chakra is often symbolised by a green lotus, mirroring the deep connection between the heart and the natural world.

As your heart opens -little by little, breath by breath—know that you are held, always, by the wild and loving arms of the earth.

The Process of Opening Our Heart

When we open our hearts—to nature, to ourselves, to life—we may find emotions rising to the surface in unexpected ways. This is natural. The heart holds not only love and joy but also sorrow, longing, and memories we may have pushed aside. In our everyday lives, we often keep these feelings contained, tucking them away beneath the weight of routine, responsibility, or distraction. But nature has a way of softening those barriers, inviting us to simply *feel*.

At first, this might feel unfamiliar, even vulnerable. As you engage in heart-opening practices, emotions may surface—sometimes gently, like a breeze shifting through the trees, other times like an unexpected wave. This chapter is not about forcing anything, but about allowing. The opening of the heart is a process of making space for whatever arises, not squashing it down or turning away as we so often do.

If a feeling stirs within you, begin simply by noticing. Just *be* with it, wrapped in nature's quiet embrace. Let the land hold you, as the earth holds the roots of every tree, steady and unshaken. And if, in time, you feel an inner strength—a quiet readiness—you can *lean into* what you feel. Allow the emotions to arise fully, to exist in your awareness without resistance. Imagine the trees bearing witness, the sky vast enough to hold all that you carry, the wind whispering that you are not alone. This is when healing is most powerful—when we stop resisting and allow it *all* to move through us.

Like a storm rolling across the sky, emotions will pass. The rain may fall heavily for a time, but afterward, the air feels lighter, the earth replenished, the world fresh with new beginnings. Trust this process. Trust that nature, in her infinite wisdom, knows how to guide you through it.

Feeling Into Your Heart: A Gentle Check-In

Before beginning the practices ahead, take a quiet moment to gently feel into your own heart. Sometimes we don't realise how guarded or open we are—especially if we've been moving through life in 'doing mode' or have learnt to protect our emotions. This isn't about judging or analysing yourself. It's simply an invitation to become curious, to check in with how your heart feels *right now*.

Find a peaceful place—outdoors, if possible—and sit or stand comfortably. Place one or both hands over your heart. Take a few slow breaths, and softly ask yourself:

- What does my heart feel like right now?
- When was the last time I felt something deeply?
- Do I allow myself space to feel, or do I tend to stay busy or distracted?
- What does my heart long for more of?
- How do I respond to beauty or stillness when I notice it in nature?

There are no right answers. Simply notice. Be gentle. Even if you feel nothing at all—*that is okay*. Sometimes, just the act of placing your hand on your heart and asking these questions begins to soften something inside. Like a flower, the heart opens best in warmth, safety, and time. Trust that your heart will bloom in its own way. Take a breath. This is where the next part of your journey begins.

Gratitude Trail Walk

Wander along a natural path and, with each step, silently express thanks for a detail you notice—a vibrant leaf, a sunlit glade, a gentle breeze. Let the landscape awaken feelings of appreciation. This practice nurtures thankfulness and deepens your connection with nature.

- Cultivates gratitude by encouraging you to notice and appreciate the details of nature.
- Enhances your connection with the environment and fosters a positive, reflective mindset.

A natural walking path such as a park, forest, or beach trail

Intention: "With every step I open my heart in gratitude, recognising the gifts that nature offers me."

Find a natural trail or pathway that feels gentle and familiar. This is not a walk for speed, but for presence and appreciation. Begin your walk slowly, letting your feet find a steady rhythm. With each step, invite your awareness to open. Notice the textures beneath your feet, the way light moves through leaves, the sound of birds or breeze. Let the landscape meet you, one moment at a time.

As you walk, begin a quiet practice of thanks. With every step, let your gaze settle on one small detail—a glistening drop of dew, a curling leaf, the scent of the earth—and silently offer your gratitude. You might think, Thank you for this colour. Thank you for this sound. Thank you for this breath.

There's no need to force it. Let your gratitude be simple and sincere, a soft conversation between your heart and the land. Let it grow naturally as you move—step by step, thanks by thanks.

By the end of your walk, you may find that something within you has shifted. Pause before you leave the trail. Stand still. Take a final deep breath and feel the gratitude you've gathered gently settle inside you—quiet, nourishing, and real.

How did expressing gratitude with each step affect your experience of the walk?
What specific details in the landscape stood out to you, and why?

Consider journalling about your experience, noting the details that brought you joy and gratitude.

Loving-Kindness

Find a sturdy, welcoming tree and sit beneath its shade. Close your eyes, feel its steady presence, and send warm, loving-kindness to yourself, the tree, and all living things around you. This practice helps deepen your sense of connection, compassion, and inner peace.

 *Outcomes*
- Cultivates a deep sense of compassion and self-kindness.
- Enhances your connection with nature and the living energy around you.

 *Items*
A sturdy tree in a peaceful outdoor setting

Intention: "I send love to myself, to others, and to all living beings."

 *Steps*

Find a tree that feels welcoming—a quiet, grounded presence that draws you in. Let it be a tree that feels like a friend. Settle yourself beneath its branches, resting in the shade it offers. Sit comfortably letting your hands rest softly in your lap or by your sides. Close your eyes or soften your gaze, and take a few deep, calming breaths.

Begin to feel the presence of the tree behind or beside you—rooted, strong, and steady. Let its quiet stillness support you, as if its calm is slowly settling into your own body. Feel the strength of its trunk, the groundedness of its roots, the openness of its branches.

Now gently turn your attention inward. Begin to offer yourself a sense of loving-kindness. You might silently say: May I be peaceful. May I be safe. May I be held in love. Let the words be simple, and let the feeling grow—like warmth gently spreading through your chest.

When you're ready, allow that feeling to expand outward. Offer this same kindness to the tree that shelters you. Then, let it ripple further still—to the birds in its branches, the creatures nearby, the plants and earth beneath you. Let your heart become a soft beacon of connection—radiating love to all that surrounds you. Stay with this gentle practice for as long as you like. When it feels complete, take one final breath and open your eyes slowly.

 *Reflect*

How did it feel to send loving-kindness to yourself and the natural world?
What sensations or emotions arose as you connected with the tree's steady presence?

 *More*

Invite a friend to share a similar practice, creating a shared moment of connection with nature.

Flower of Forgiveness

Choose a delicate wildflower and hold it gently in your hand. As you admire its beauty, visualise it absorbing any lingering resentment or hurt. This practice encourages a deep emotional release and nurtures compassion for yourself and others.

 **Outcomes**
- Enhances mindfulness and emotional healing through a tactile connection
- Encourages the practise of forgiveness by symbolically releasing negative feelings.

 **Items**
A delicate wildflower found in nature (or a similar natural flower)

Intention: "I soften and let go, offering forgiveness to myself and others."

 **Steps**

Wander gently through nature until a delicate wildflower catches your eye—one that seems to call to you, even in its quietness. Let it be one that speaks to your heart. Settle nearby in a peaceful spot, where you can sit and be still with it.

Gently hold the wildflower in your hand or simply rest your gaze upon it. Take a few deep, calming breaths, letting yourself arrive fully in this moment. Let the beauty of the flower draw you in—its soft petals, its intricate design, the way it leans toward the light.

As you sit, begin to imagine the flower as a vessel of transformation. Visualise it gently absorbing anything heavy you may be carrying—resentment, old wounds, unspoken words. You don't need to force anything. Just breathe, and allow the flower to receive what you're ready to release. With each breath, see the flower becoming more vibrant, more luminous—glowing with your willingness to forgive, to soften, to heal. Let its presence remind you of your own resilience and tenderness.

Stay here for a few minutes, breathing gently, letting the energy of the flower work quietly within you. Let forgiveness be a process that blooms slowly, in its own time. When you feel ready, offer the flower back to the land—placing it gently on the earth—or keep it close as a symbol of your strength, your heart, and your choice to open once again.

 **Reflect**
How did holding and visualising the wildflower affect your emotional state?
What sensations or thoughts arose as you practised letting go of negative feelings?

 **More**
Create a small piece of art or poetry inspired by the wildflower and the feelings of forgiveness it evoked.

Sunset of Love

As the day fades into evening, sit with an unobstructed view of the sunset. Let the shifting colours remind you of life's beauty, and reflect on the love that fills your heart—letting it expand with every changing hue.

- Cultivates mindfulness by connecting you with the natural beauty of the sunset.
- Encourages emotional reflection and the expansion of love and gratitude.

A location with an unobstructed view of the sunset

Intention: "As the sun sets, I reflect on love and how I can welcome more of it into my life."

Find a place where you can watch the sunset unfold.. Wherever you are, let it be somewhere you can sit in stillness and watch the sky slowly shift from day to night. Settle into a comfortable seat and take a few deep, calming breaths. Let your body soften. Let your thoughts slow. With each breath, allow yourself to arrive more fully in this present moment.

Turn your gaze toward the horizon and let your eyes rest gently on the colours that begin to appear—shades of gold, rose, violet, and blue. Watch how they change moment by moment, blending and fading with grace. There's no rush here. Just allow yourself to receive it all.

As you sit with the sky, let the beauty of the sunset stir something in your heart. Let it remind you of the love you hold—for people, for places, for life itself. With each breath, feel your heart expanding gently, as if the colours of the sky are blooming inside you.

You might recall a joyful memory, a moment of kindness, or simply sit in the quiet warmth of appreciation. Let the sunset be a mirror, reflecting the love and beauty already within you.

Stay in this space for as long as the light lingers. When the colours finally soften into twilight, take one last deep breath.

How did the sunset influence your mood and sense of love?
What colours or changes in the sky resonated with you the most?

Consider journalling your reflections or creating a piece of art inspired by the sunset's colours .

Forgiveness Flow

Choose a spot by a gently flowing stream or a calm lake. Watch the water's unhurried course and use it as a mirror for your emotions—allowing old hurts to wash away as you offer forgiveness to yourself and others.

 *Outcomes*
- Cultivates mindfulness through deep sensory observation and emotional reflection.
- Encourages the release of old hurts and the practice of forgiveness.

 *Items*

A serene outdoor location by a gently flowing stream or a lake.

Intention: "I allow the natural world to guide me in releasing old wounds."

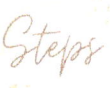 *Steps*

Find a peaceful spot beside a flowing stream, river, or calm shoreline. Let your body settle into a comfortable seat, and take a few slow, grounding breaths. Feel the earth beneath you, the movement of air around you, and the flow of life in this moment.

Turn your attention to the water. Watch how it moves—fluid, effortless, never resisting. Listen to its voice—the soft splash, the ripple, the hush of flow. As you sit with the water, gently bring to mind any lingering emotions or old hurts that have weighed on your heart. You don't need to analyse or hold onto them—just acknowledge what's there. Let it be present without judgement.

Now, imagine offering these feelings to the water. Not to cast them away in anger or urgency, but as a soft release. With each exhale, allow yourself to let go a little—sending out forgiveness like ripples across the surface. Forgiveness for others. Forgiveness for yourself.

Visualise the water receiving it all—washing it clean, carrying it forward, transforming pain into peace with every passing current. Remain in this gentle space for as long as you need. Let the water remind you of your own capacity to release, to soften, to begin again. When you're ready, take a final breath, offer a quiet thank you, and carry the calm with you—flowing gently back into your life.

 *Reflect*

How did observing the water influence your emotional state?
What feelings arose as you visualised old hurts being washed away?

 *More*

Take a gentle walk along the water's edge, deepening your connection to nature and your emotional healing.

Wild Love Letters

Bring a small notebook outdoors and write a short letter expressing love or gratitude to someone (or even to nature itself). Let the surroundings inspire sincere words from your heart. Deepen your connection with the world around you and cultivate gratitude.

 *Outcomes*
- Encourages mindfulness and emotional expression through writing.
- Fosters gratitude and connection with both people and nature.

 *Items*
A notebook or journal, pen
A peaceful outdoor setting

Intention: "I express my love and appreciation for the wild world, knowing that my words carry energy."

 *Steps*

Find a quiet place outdoors that stirs something in your heart—a sun-dappled grove, a spot near water, or a patch of earth beneath your favourite tree. Let it be somewhere that feels peaceful, comforting, and alive with beauty. Sit down with your notebook and pen. Before writing anything, take a few deep, slow breaths. Feel your body settle. Let your senses open to the landscape around you—the scent of the air, the sounds of birds, the quality of the light.

Now bring to mind someone or something you love. It might be a person, a cherished memory, or even nature itself. Feel the warmth of that connection as it rises within you.

Begin to write a letter from this space of love and gratitude. Don't worry about formality or structure. Just let your pen move. You might write, Thank you for... or I remember when... or simply describe how this connection makes you feel. Let your surroundings inspire you.

Write freely and honestly, without editing or overthinking. This is a love letter from your heart, not meant to impress but to express. When your letter feels complete, pause. Read it over slowly, soaking in your own words. Notice the warmth it carries, the truth it holds. Let it be a reminder of how deeply you can feel—and how easily nature can help bring that love to the surface. You might tuck the letter away or leave it as an offering.

 *Reflect*
How did writing your letter in nature influence your feelings of gratitude and connection?
What aspects of your surroundings inspired the words you chose?

 *More*
Consider sharing it with the person it's addressed to, or keep it as a personal reminder of the love in your life.

Gratitude Circle

If you're with others, form a small circle and take turns sharing what you appreciate about the natural world. If you're alone, speak these thoughts aloud letting the open air carry your gratitude. This mindful practice nurtures gratitude and deepens your connection with nature.

 **Outcomes**
- Cultivates gratitude by encouraging you to notice and appreciate nature's beauty.
- Fosters a sense of community and connection, whether with others or with the natural world.

 **Items**
A quiet outdoor setting. A small group of people for a shared experience.

Intention: "I give thanks for the people, places, and moments that fill my heart."

 **Steps**

Find your way to a peaceful outdoor space. If you're practising with a group, form a small circle—standing or sitting, whatever feels natural. If you're alone, simply find a spot where you can feel grounded and at ease. Take a few deep, steady breaths to arrive in the moment. Let your body soften and your attention settle.

When you're ready, begin by sharing something you feel grateful for in the natural world. Speak it aloud—whether it's the golden warmth of the sun or the coolness of the breeze. Let your words be simple and sincere.

If you're with others, listen closely as each person shares—pausing between offerings to hold space for their gratitude. If you're alone, let your voice carry gently into the air, as if speaking directly to the land itself. There is something powerful in voicing thanks where the trees, the sky, and the earth can hear it. You might choose to go around the circle more than once, or linger in silence between sharings. Let the rhythm unfold naturally. There's no need to rush.

As the practice draws to a close, pause together—or within yourself—and feel the energy that's been created. This web of appreciation, gently woven between you and the natural world, is a quiet kind of magic. Let it fill you.

 **Reflect**
How did sharing your appreciation for nature affect your mood and sense of presence?
How did the experience influence your connection with others or with nature itself?

 **More**
Combine this with a mindful nature walk, pausing along the way to express your thanks for the beauty you encounter.

Earth's Heartbeat

Tune into the subtle sounds of nature. Imagine that each rustle or distant call is part of the earth's own heartbeat—resonating with your inner rhythm. This mindful practice invites you to connect deeply with the natural pulse of life and cultivate a sense of calm.

 *Outcomes*
- Enhances your sensory awareness and deepens your connection with nature.
- Encourages mindfulness and inner calm by aligning with the earth's natural rhythms.

 *Items*
A quiet outdoor space with a soft natural surface (such as grass or sand)

Intention: "I place my hand on the earth - reminding me that I am always supported and never alone."

 *Steps*

Find a peaceful outdoor spot where you can sit or lie down comfortably. Let the ground support you fully. Take a few slow, deep breaths, allowing your body to soften and your attention to gently arrive in this place.

Close your eyes, or let your gaze soften. Begin to listen—really listen. Notice the subtle sounds surrounding you: the rustle of leaves above, the whisper of wind moving through trees, a bird calling in the distance, the hum of insects nearby. Let these sounds rise and fall like waves, without trying to name or follow them.

Now imagine that each sound you hear is part of something greater—a rhythm, a pulse, a quiet beating that belongs to the earth itself. Let yourself feel the resonance of this rhythm. Imagine that the land is breathing with you, the earth's own heartbeat is gently aligning with your own.

Let yourself rest in this stillness. Not doing, just being. Let the natural world hold you in its steady pulse. With every breath, feel more connected, more grounded, more in tune with the great rhythm of life around and within you. Stay in this quiet awareness for as long as it feels right. When you're ready to move, take a final deep breath, open your eyes slowly, and carry this steady presence with you.

 *Reflect*
How did tuning into the earth's heartbeat affect your sense of calm? What sensations or emotions arose as you listened to the natural sounds around you?

 *More*
Try this practice at different times of day to observe how the earth's heartbeat shifts with the changing light.

Birdsong of Joy

Listen to the lively chorus of birds at dawn or dusk. Let their joyful calls remind you of the innate happiness within, encouraging you to reconnect with your own inner cheer. This practice invites you to reconnect with your inner cheer, brightening your spirit.

- Cultivates a sense of joy and inner cheer through mindful listening.
- Enhances sensory awareness by focusing on the natural sounds of birds.

A natural setting, ideally at dawn or dusk

Intention: "I listen to the songs of the birds and allow their joy to spark my own."

Find a quiet spot outdoors where the sounds of birds are clear—perhaps early in the morning or just before dusk, when their songs rise in joyful chorus. Let yourself settle into the space. Take a few slow, grounding breaths. Let your body soften and your awareness open.

Begin to tune in to the birdsong around you. You might hear a single call or a layered chorus—each one carrying its own rhythm, melody, and tone. Don't try to identify or interpret. Just listen, like you would to a beautiful piece of music, letting the sound move through you.

Let these songs be more than background noise. Let them lift something inside you. Imagine each call as a reminder of the joy that lives within you—the untamed, light-hearted, effortless cheer that sometimes lies buried under thought and routine.

As you listen, feel this joy begin to stir. Maybe it's a smile, a warmth in your chest, or simply a sense of lightness. Let the birds remind you how natural it is to sing, to express, to simply be alive. Remain here, breathing and listening, for as long as you like. When the moment feels complete, take one last breath and thank the birds—out loud or silently—for sharing their joy. Carry that spark with you into the rest of your day.

How did the sound of birdsong influence your mood and sense of joy? What sensations or feelings arose as you immersed yourself in nature's chorus?

Consider journalling about your experience, noting any changes in your mood or outlook.

Rock Patience

Sit with a rock in your palm, sensing its stillness and age. In this practice, you hold a rock in your palm and focus on its enduring stillness. As you connect with its texture, weight, and coolness, allow its timeless presence to ground you.

 **Outcomes**
- Deepens your sensory awareness and mindfulness through tactile connection.
- Encourages patience and reflection by focusing on the rock's enduring qualities.

 **Items**
A rock that calls to you, ideally one with interesting texture or history.

Intention: "I embrace the patience of the earth knowing that time brings understanding, and wisdom."

 **Steps**

Wander slowly through a natural place and let your attention be drawn to a single rock—one that seems to speak to you in its quiet way. Let it feel right in your hand. Settle in comfortably and take a few deep, steady breaths. Place the rock in your palm and simply hold it. Notice its texture—rough or worn smooth by time. Feel its weight, its coolness, its quiet presence in your hand.

This rock has been here a long time—shaped by earth, weather, and time itself. It carries patience in its very being. Let yourself feel that patience. Let it move into your own body like an echo, helping you slow down, soften, and be present.

Sit quietly for a while allowing the stillness of the rock to inspire stillness within you. If thoughts arise, return to the weight in your hand, the way the stone rests without resistance. There's no rush. No expectation. Just the steady presence of something ancient and calm.

When you feel ready, lift your gaze and return to your surroundings. You might choose to keep the rock as a reminder of groundedness—or place it back on the earth with quiet thanks. Either way, carry its calm with you as you move gently through the rest of your day.

 **Reflect**
How did holding the rock affect your sense of patience and stillness? What sensations did you notice in your hand and mind as you focused on the rock?

 **More**
Consider keeping the rock in a special place at home or in your garden as a reminder of patience and resilience.

Sun's Embrace

Feel and be with the sun, connecting with its energy and warmth. Allow yourself to fully immerse in the sensation of its energy. This mindful practise invites you to connect deeply with the natural energy of the sun, cultivating presence and radiance from within.

 *Outcomes*
- Enhances sensory awareness by focusing on the sun's warmth and energy.
- Encourages mindfulness by aligning your inner presence with the vitality of the sun.

 *Items*
Outdoor space with sunlight (preferably during a gentle period such as early morning or late afternoon)

Intention: "I welcome the warmth of the sun, feeling its radiant energy fill my heart with vitality."

 *Steps*

Find a peaceful spot outdoors where sunlight reaches you—perhaps a clearing, a garden, or a quiet place near a window. Sit or stand in a way that allows the sun to gently touch your skin. Let yourself arrive slowly, feeling the space around you and beneath you.

Close your eyes or soften your gaze, and take a few deep, steady breaths. With each inhale, let your body relax a little more. With each exhale, let go of whatever you've been carrying. There is nowhere else to be.

Begin to notice the warmth of the sun on your skin. Feel where it lands—on your face, your shoulders, your hands. Let yourself fully receive its heat and light, not just as a sensation, but as nourishment. With each breath, imagine the sunlight moving into your body—filling you with golden energy, softening your muscles, lighting you from the inside out. Let this warmth awaken your inner vitality. Let it remind you of your own radiance, always present beneath the surface.

Remain in this quiet presence for as long as it feels right. Let the sun hold you. Let it connect you to the present moment, to your breath, to your aliveness. When you're ready, take one final deep inhale, and exhale slowly with gratitude—for the warmth, for the light, and for this moment of connection with the living sky.

Reflect
How did feeling the sun's warmth influence your sense of energy and calm?
What sensations or emotions arose as you connected with the sun's energy?

 *More*
Draw or write about the sensations, emotions, and any insights that emerged from connecting with the sun.

Nature's Beauty

Beauty in nature is everywhere—sometimes in grand landscapes, sometimes in the smallest details. This practice invites you to pause and fully take in something that moves you, letting yourself be filled with wonder and appreciation.

- Cultivates deep appreciation and presence through focused observation.
- Encourages emotional openness by allowing beauty to touch the heart.

A natural setting or object that sparks joy.

Intention: "I open my heart to the beauty around me, allowing it to remind me of the beauty within me."

Step outside with no agenda, no destination—just a willingness to be drawn toward something beautiful. Walk slowly, or simply stand and let your gaze wander until something catches your attention. It might be a single flower swaying in the breeze or the way sunlight dances through the leaves. Let it be whatever stirs your heart.

When you've found it, settle nearby and make yourself comfortable. Allow your breath to slow as you rest your attention on this one moment of beauty.

Observe closely—notice the details. The shades of colour, the textures, the way light touches it. Let your eyes move slowly, with reverence. This is not about thinking or naming—just witnessing. Just being with.

With each breath, let that beauty fill you. Feel it soften the edges of your day. Let it expand within your chest, opening your heart to wonder. If emotions arise—delight, awe, gratitude—let them move through you like sunlight through leaves. There is nothing to fix or change. Just feel.

Remain here for as long as the moment holds you. When you feel complete, take one final deep breath, and silently offer your thanks—to the flower, the branch, the light, the life—for reminding you of the beauty that still surrounds you… and lives within you.

What did you notice when you gave your full attention to nature's beauty? How did this experience affect your emotions and sense of connection?

Try capturing this moment in a creative way—write a short reflection, take a photo, sketch what you saw, or describe the experience in a poem.

A Moment of Reflection

As you prepare to move forward, take a moment to reflect on your journey into the heart.

How did opening your heart to nature feel? Did you experience moments of connection, tenderness, or expansion?
_____
_____
_____

What emotions surfaced for you during these practices? Were there moments of joy, gratitude, or even vulnerability?
_____
_____
_____

How did the heart-centred practices influence your sense of belonging? Did you feel a greater connection to yourself, to the land, or to others?
_____
_____
_____

Was it challenging to lean into your emotions? How did you navigate any resistance, and what helped you soften into the experience?
_____
_____
_____

Do you feel ready to move forward? The next chapter invites you to awaken your senses and deepen your connection with nature through touch, scent, sound, and feeling. Does this feel like a natural next step, or would you like to spend more time in the heart space?

Move gently, at your own pace. The journey is yours to unfold.

Chapter 4:
Awaken Your Senses

*In the quiet of dawn, let your eyes open wide,
to the gentle brush of sunlight over dew-kissed leaves.
Hear the soft murmur of the breeze whispering secrets
through ancient branches and waking the stillness.*

*Feel the cool caress of morning air on your skin,
each gust a reminder of nature's tender embrace.
Taste the promise of fresh earth as you breathe in deeply,
savouring the tang of life and renewal.*

*Smell the wild perfume of blossoming flowers and rich soil,
a fragrant symphony that stirs forgotten memories.
Let yourself be fully alive in this sensory dance,
where each touch, sight, sound, and scent
unfolds the wonder of the world around you.*

Into the Senses: Embodied Presence

With presence as your anchor, breath as your rhythm, and heart as your compass, the next step on your Wild Stillness journey brings you into the living landscape of the senses. This is where awareness becomes embodied—where the practice moves from quiet internal reflection into *vivid, sensory connection* with the world around you.

Your senses are the gateways between inner and outer experience. They are always offering you ways to return to the moment—through the scent of eucalyptus after rain, the coolness of soil under your fingertips, the sound of wind moving through dry grass, the tang of salt air on your lips. These are not small details; they are *invitations*—each one a thread pulling you gently back to the here and now.

The previous chapters have been about building the inner foundation—cultivating stillness, grounding, and emotional openness. Now, those core practices support you in expanding outward again, this time with *heightened awareness*. With a steady breath and an open heart, you can begin to truly *feel* the world—not just mentally or emotionally, but through the raw, direct experience of touch, sound, smell, and taste.

The Senses and Nature in Ancient Wisdom

Long before the modern concept of mindfulness, ancient cultures around the world deeply understood the importance of the senses in connecting with the natural world—and with the sacred. The senses weren't seen as distractions or obstacles to enlightenment; they were honoured as *pathways* to insight, presence, and union with something greater than the self.

In Indigenous Australian cultures, sensory connection to Country is fundamental. Every sound, scent, and shift in the landscape carries meaning. Knowledge is passed down not just through words, but through songlines, movement, and observation. The land is alive, and listening—truly listening.

In Hindu and yogic traditions, the five senses (*indriyas*) are closely linked to the five elements (*mahabhutas*), each one a bridge between the outer world and the inner self. Practices like *pratyahara* (sensory withdrawal) aren't about numbing the senses, but about refining them—so we become *more* attuned, not less. The scent of sandalwood, the sound of a mantra, the flicker of flame—all are used as tools to focus awareness and awaken deeper states of consciousness.

In Buddhist teachings, awareness of sensory experience is a key foundation of mindfulness. Noticing the fleeting nature of sound, smell, taste, or touch teaches us about impermanence. In Zen practice, everyday acts—like drinking tea or sweeping the floor—are approached with full sensory presence, turning the ordinary into something sacred.

Across ancient traditions, the senses were never separate from spirituality or wellbeing—they were *integral*. The scent of smoke from a sacred fire, the texture of earth beneath bare feet, the sound of birdsong at dawn—these were ways to commune with the divine, to ground into the present, and to receive the wisdom of the living world.

The Senses as Pathways to Deep Connection

Your senses are always with you—quiet companions that gently guide you back to the present moment, no matter where you are. You don't need to be deep in the forest to return to presence; you can simply pause and feel the breeze on your skin, listen to the sound around you, or notice the scent in the air. In busy moments or stressful days, your senses offer a doorway back to stillness. They're always here, waiting for your attention, ready to reconnect you with the world—and with yourself.

However, many of us go through life dulled to our senses, caught in our thoughts, or numbed by routine. This chapter is a chance to reawaken—to engage with nature not just as something you observe, but something you *interact with intimately*. Through the senses, the world becomes alive again. And so do you.

We use our senses every day—often without even realising it. We hear, but do we truly *listen*? We touch, but do we fully *feel*? We smell, but do we pause to *notice* what that scent stirs within us? In daily life, our senses are often dulled by distraction, busyness, and overstimulation. But when we bring mindful awareness to them—especially in nature—they awaken with new depth and meaning.

Nature invites us to slow down and sense more *deeply*. To *listen* not just with our ears, but with our presence—with our whole body and our heart. To feel the vibration of birdsong echoing inside us, or the way the rustle of leaves can shift our state of being. When we listen deeply, we begin to hear the language of the land—not in words, but in rhythm, in texture, in tone.

To truly *see* is not only to observe, but to *witness*. When we are present, we begin to notice the way light filters through leaves, the fine detail of a feather, or the subtle shimmer of dew on grass. These are the small, quiet miracles that are so often missed when our minds are elsewhere.

Touch becomes a form of communication—bare feet on warm stone, the soft give of moss, the dry, peeling bark of a eucalypt beneath your hand. Smell connects us instantly to memory and mood—the scent of crushed leaves, sun-warmed earth, the rain on dry ground. Even taste becomes richer when we mindfully sip tea made from foraged herbs or taste the salt air on our lips.

When the senses are fully engaged, something within us opens. We become more *alive*, more present, more connected. The boundary between ourselves and the natural world begins to dissolve. We are no longer just visitors in nature—we are participants, listening, feeling, and remembering who we are.

Through the practices in this chapter, you'll be invited to slow down and engage with your senses in a whole new way. Not just as tools for survival or function, but as *gateways*—to presence, to awe, to meaning, and to the deep stillness that lives within the wild.

Nature's Symphony

Focus on the layered sounds around you—the rustle of leaves, distant birdcalls, the whisper of the wind—and let each sound invite you deeper into the present. This mindful exercise helps you appreciate the richness of nature's auditory landscape.

- Enhances your mindfulness by developing deep listening skills and sensory awareness.
- Encourages a connection with nature through the appreciation of its sounds.

A quiet outdoor setting where you can comfortably sit or stand

Intention: "I open my ears, allowing the sounds of nature to bring me fully into the present moment."

Find a quiet place in nature where you won't be disturbed—somewhere you can sit or stand comfortably and simply listen. Close your eyes if you like, or soften your gaze, and begin by taking a few deep, grounding breaths. Let your body settle, and awareness to gently open.

Now begin to listen. Notice the layers of sound that surround you. The rustling of leaves above, the rhythmic chirp of birds, the distant hum of insects, or the whisper of wind moving through branches. Let each sound arrive on its own, without needing to name it or chase it.

Allow these sounds to draw you into the present moment. Notice the subtle shifts in tone and rhythm. Some sounds may come and go, others may remain like a steady hum beneath it all. Listen as if the land is singing to you. Let it touch your awareness and invite you deeper into connection. If your mind wanders, gently bring your attention back to sound.

Stay with this listening for several minutes, simply being present with what you hear. When you're ready, open your eyes slowly. Take a breath. You've just awakened one of your most ancient senses—tuned in to the earth's quiet music. Let it echo in you as you return to the day.

How did the layered sounds of nature affect your sense of calm and presence?
What specific sounds stood out to you, and how did they influence your inner state?

Try this practice at different times of day to explore how the natural symphony changes with light and weather.

Scented Wander

Stroll along a natural trail with an open heart. Pause periodically to inhale deeply, noticing the earthy aroma of damp soil, wild herbs, or the delicate fragrance of blossoms. This practice encourages you to connect with your environment through the sense of smell.

 *Outcomes*
- Enhances your sensory awareness by inviting you to focus on the natural scents around you.
- Encourages emotional openness through the act of deep, reflective breathing.

 *Items*
A natural trail or outdoor path with rich, varied scents

Intention: "I invite nature's aromas to awaken my senses and deepen my connection to the living world."

 *Steps*

Step onto a trail or natural path where you feel relaxed and at home—somewhere the land feels alive beneath your feet and the air is rich with subtle fragrances. Let this be a gentle walk, not to arrive anywhere, but to awaken your sense of smell.

Begin walking slowly, allowing your attention to stay close to the earth. Notice the feel of the ground beneath your feet, the breeze on your skin, the rustling leaves or birdsong in the distance. Keep your awareness soft and curious.

Now and then, pause wherever you feel drawn. Maybe it's a patch of herbs, a rain-dampened tree, or a cluster of blossoms. Close your eyes if you'd like, and take a slow, deep breath through your nose. Let the scent come to you. Breathe it in fully.

Notice what you smell. Is it earthy and rich like soil? Sweet like blossoms? Sharp like eucalyptus or pine? Let the scent settle into you. Don't overthink it—just feel how it stirs your memory, your body, your connection to place.

With each inhale, receive. With each exhale, let go. Allow this practice to bring calm and presence, one breath at a time. Continue walking in this way—pausing, breathing, noticing—as long as you like. Let scent guide your awareness, reminding you how intimately we belong to the land through the simplest, most ancient of senses.

 *Reflect*

How did focusing on the scents of nature influence your overall experience? What emotions or memories were evoked by the different aromas?

 *More*

Create a small scent collection by gathering pressed wild herbs or leaves.

Barefoot Connection

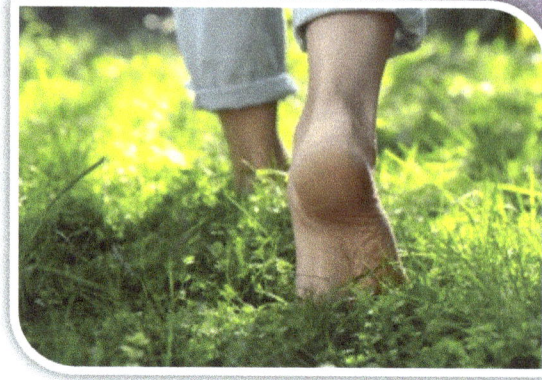

Feel the textures beneath your feet and let the sensations ground you, connecting you with the pulse of the land. As you focus on the coolness of the grass, the warmth of the sand, or the firmness of the soil, you become deeply present and connected to the natural world.

Outcomes
- Cultivates sensory mindfulness by engaging directly with natural textures.
- Enhances your connection with the environment and grounds you in the present.

Items
A natural outdoor surface such as grass, sand, or earth

Intention: "With every step I feel the earth beneath me, grounding myself in the embrace of nature."

Steps

Find a safe and welcoming patch of earth where you can remove your shoes and feel the land beneath you—perhaps a grassy lawn, a stretch of sand, a forest floor, or soft soil after rain. Let this be your invitation to awaken through the soles of your feet.

Take a moment as you remove your shoes and socks. Feel the shift—from protected and cushioned to open and sensing. Stand still for a breath or two, letting your feet settle into this new contact with the natural world.

Begin to walk slowly, letting each step land with full awareness. Feel the coolness of grass, the warmth of sun-soaked ground, the texture of small stones or shifting grains of sand. Notice how your feet adjust—how the body responds, how each surface brings something different.

With every step, let yourself feel more grounded. The earth is steady beneath you, always here, always holding you. Let your awareness rest in the sensations—the slight pressure, the temperature, the tickle of a blade of grass or the firmness of packed earth. There's no destination. This is a walk of presence. Continue for as long as feels good, letting your connection deepen, step by step. When you're ready, pause. Stand still. Take a deep breath, and feel the way the land has welcomed you—just as you are, barefoot and fully alive.

Reflect
How did the different textures beneath your feet influence your sense of presence?
What sensations or emotions arose as you connected directly with the earth?

More
Explore different natural settings—such as a forest floor or beach.

Herbal Touch

Gather a few leaves, petals, or herbs and explore their textures. Let the natural patterns and softness or roughness awaken your tactile awareness. This practice invites you to awaken your sense of touch and deepen your connection with nature's details.

- Enhances your sensory awareness and tactile mindfulness with natural elements.
- Encourages appreciation of nature's diverse textures and patterns.

A small collection of leaves, petals, or herbs

Intention: "I explore the textures of nature, allowing my hands to experience the language of the land."

Find your way to a place in nature where you can safely and respectfully gather a few natural treasures—perhaps some soft petals, textured leaves, or aromatic herbs. Before collecting anything, pause. Look around. Feel the stillness of the land and ask quietly for permission. Take only what is abundant, and always with care.

As you begin, move slowly. Let your eyes land on something that draws your attention. Gently gather a few pieces—maybe a fuzzy leaf, a sprig of rosemary, or a velvety petal. Hold one in your hand and simply explore. Feel its texture—run your fingers across its surface. Is it soft? Smooth? Prickly or veined? Notice the edges, the weight, the moisture or dryness. Let your sense of touch lead you into deeper presence.

Spend time with each item you've gathered. Let the simple act of touching reconnect you to the natural world in an intimate, wordless way. This is how we once knew the land—through our fingertips, through our senses.

Take your time. When you're finished, return the pieces gently to the earth. Walk away with a heightened sense of connection remembering how much can be felt in the simplest touch.

How did exploring the textures of natural items influence your sense of touch and presence?
What sensations or memories did different textures evoke for you?

Consider creating a simple art piece, such as a collage or a pressed herb arrangement.

Soil Grounding

Gently press your hand into the earth, feeling its cool, rich texture. Reflect on how this simple act connects you to the ground beneath you and the life it sustains. This mindful practice invites you to ground yourself, both physically and emotionally.

 *Outcomes*
- Cultivates sensory awareness through direct tactile connection with the earth.
- Encourages mindfulness by drawing your attention to the present moment.

 *Items*
A natural outdoor area with exposed soil (a garden, park, or natural trail)

Intention: "I press my hands into the earth, feeling its stability and quiet wisdom flow through me."

 *Steps*

Find a quiet spot outdoors where the soil is bare and welcoming. Take off your shoes if you'd like and allow your feet to rest directly on the ground. Then lower yourself so you can reach the soil easily. Gently place your hand on the earth's surface, letting your fingers spread across its texture.

Feel what's beneath your palm—the coolness, the grains, the firmness. Notice any dampness, small stones, or roots beneath your touch. Let your awareness gather fully into your hand, into this moment of contact.

Close your eyes and begin to breathe slowly. With each inhale, sense the quiet strength of the earth beneath you. With each exhale, let your body settle a little more—allowing any tension to release into the ground.

Imagine the soil as a steady presence—ancient, alive, and endlessly supportive. Reflect on how this very earth nourishes trees, holds rivers, grows food. And here it is, holding you too.

Stay in this grounded stillness for as long as it feels right. When you're ready, lift your hand slowly and thank the earth in your own way. Carry this connection with you as you return to your day—rooted, calm, and gently held by the land.

 *Reflect*
How did feeling the soil beneath your hand influence your sense of presence and grounding?
What sensations or emotions arose as you connected with the earth?

 *More*
Consider journalling about the experience, noting any changes in your mood or perspective.

Treasure Hunt

Wander through a natural setting and collect small items (like a smooth stone or a textured leaf) that capture your interest. Take time to feel and appreciate each object's unique qualities. This mindful practice helps you deepen your connection with nature.

 *Outcomes*
- Enhances your sensory awareness by engaging your sense of touch.
- Cultivates mindfulness as you focus on the unique qualities of each natural object.

 *Items*
- A natural outdoor setting such as a park, forest, or beach

Intention: "I move through nature with playful curiosity noticing the small wonders that reveal themselves."

 *Steps*

Wander into a natural space that feels gentle and familiar. Let your pace be slow and your senses wide open, especially the sense of touch. As you move, let your eyes and hands guide you. Maybe a smooth stone catches the light just right, or a leaf with intricate veins invites your fingers. Perhaps a fallen petal, soft and bright, draws your gaze. When something captures your interest, pause. Hold it gently, feel its texture, and if it feels right, carry it with you. Only take what's fallen, and leave plenty behind for the land to thrive.

After gathering a few treasures, find a quiet place to sit. Lay them out in front of you or hold them one by one. Let your fingers explore each surface. Is it cool? Rough? Silky? Grainy? Feel the weight in your palm, the edges, the temperature. Let yourself linger.

Each object has its own story, shaped by weather, time, and place. Reflect on what drew you to each one. Was it colour? Shape? A feeling? Let that sense of curiosity and connection deepen. You're not just collecting things—you're collecting moments of wonder.

Stay here for a little while, appreciating these small gifts from nature. When you're ready, return any items you don't need to the land with care. Let the tactile memory stay with you—a reminder of how alive and intricate the natural world truly is, and how close you can feel to it, simply through the palm of your hand.

 *Reflect*
How did exploring the textures of natural objects affect your awareness of the environment?
What feelings or memories did the different items evoke for you?

 *More*
Consider creating a small collage or art piece with the items you collected.

Earth's Vibrations

Focus on the subtle vibrations from the ground—the hum of life beneath you—and feel how it mirrors your own inner pulse. This mindful engagement helps you connect with the ground's rhythm and how it mirrors your inner pulse, fostering a deep sense of grounding.

 **Outcomes**
- Cultivates sensory mindfulness by connecting you with the earth's natural vibrations.
- Enhances awareness of your inner pulse and emotional state.

 **Items**
A quiet outdoor area with a soft patch of grass

Intention: "I tune into the subtle hum of the earth feeling the quiet energy that connects all living things

 **Steps**

Find a peaceful patch of grass where you can sit or lie down with ease. Let yourself arrive slowly, taking in the sights and sounds around you until your body begins to settle. Place one hand gently over your heart. Close your eyes, and take a few deep, calming breaths. With each inhale, let your awareness drop further into your body. With each exhale, feel the ground rising up to meet you.

Now turn your attention toward the earth beneath you. Sense into the subtle vibrations—the hum of insects, the distant flutter of wings, the pulse of life moving below the surface. Even in stillness, the earth is alive. As you breathe, imagine your own heartbeat gently syncing with this rhythm. Let yourself feel part of something older, deeper, and steady. Maybe you notice a warmth in your chest, or a quiet calm spreading through your body. Let it all be welcome.

Stay in this felt connection for as long as it feels nourishing. There's no need to understand it—just feel. Let the quiet beat of the earth remind you of your own steady presence, your place in this web of life. When you're ready, take one last deep breath. Gently open your eyes, holding the echo of the earth's gentle rhythm within you.

Reflect
How did focusing on the earth's vibrations influence your sense of grounding and presence?
What did you notice about the connection between the earth's pulse and your own heartbeat?

More
Try this practice at different times of day to explore how the earth's vibrations and your inner sensations change with the environment.

Scented Memory

Choose a natural aroma—like the musk of pine or the crisp scent of eucalyptus—and let it evoke a memory or feeling. This practice invites you to explore how scents can unlock memories and emotions, grounding you in the present while bridging you to your past.

Outcomes
- Enhances sensory mindfulness by inviting you to focus on the sense of smell.
- Encourages emotional reflection by linking natural aromas to personal memories.

Items
A natural aromatic item

Intention: "I breathe in deeply, letting nature's scents unlock memories and emotions."

Steps

Wander gently through nature until a scent draws you in—perhaps the sweet perfume of a wildflower, the crispness of eucalyptus leaves, the earthiness of damp soil, or the sun-warmed scent of pine. Choose one natural item that feels inviting and bring it close to your nose. Inhale slowly, letting the aroma fill your senses. Don't rush—let the scent arrive like a story unfolding. Notice the details of its character—is it sharp, floral, musky, sweet? Let it linger.

As you continue breathing in the fragrance, pay attention to what arises. Does a memory bubble to the surface? A place, a person, a moment from long ago? Or maybe it stirs a feeling—comfort, longing, joy, calm. Whatever comes, welcome it with curiosity and kindness.

Let the scent guide you into presence. Stay with it for several minutes, breathing gently, allowing this quiet sensory moment to deepen your connection to yourself and to the natural world. If you feel drawn, explore other scents nearby. Each will carry its own emotional note, like different songs in nature's symphony. When you're ready, gently place the item back or keep it as a fragrant reminder of this mindful moment. Carry the memory—and the scent's quiet magic—with you as you return to your day.

Reflect
How did the chosen scent influence your mood or emotional state?
What memories or feelings did the aroma evoke for you?

More
Create a small collection of natural scented items that remind you of moments of joy.

Water Whisper

Sit by a stream, river, or pond. Focus on the gentle sound of water as it flows, splashes, or ripples, allowing its cadence to harmonise with your inner rhythm. This mindful practice helps you achieve a state of calm, connecting you deeply with the energy of the water.

 *Outcomes*
- Enhances your sensory awareness by attuning you to the subtle sounds of water.
- Encourages mindfulness and inner calm through focused listening.

 *Items*
An outdoor spot by a stream, river, or pond

Intention: "I listen to the voice of water, feeling its movement remind me of life's natural flow."

 *Steps*

Find your way to a quiet spot beside water—a stream, river, lake, or even a small pond. Settle into a comfortable seat and take a few deep, steady breaths. Feel yourself arrive—your body grounded, your mind softening. Allow your awareness to begin opening to the soundscape around you.

Now turn your full attention to the water. Listen closely. Is it flowing gently, lapping at the shore, or trickling over stones? Notice its rhythm—the pauses, the swells, the patterns of movement. Let yourself be drawn in.

As you listen, begin to feel how the sound of the water mirrors something inside you. Maybe your breath begins to flow in time with the ripples, or your thoughts settle like pebbles beneath the surface. Let the water's voice guide you—not to do anything, but simply to be.

Let go into this sound. Let it soften the edges of your mind. Let it lull you into stillness.

Remain in this gentle listening for as long as it feels good. When you're ready, take one final deep breath and open your eyes slowly. Walk away with the water's calm still echoing in you—fluid, grounded, and at peace.

 *Reflect*
How did listening to the water affect your sense of calm and presence?
What sensations or emotions did you experience as you aligned your inner rhythm with the flow of the water?

 *More*
Try this practice at different times of day to observe how the water's sounds and energy change.

Nature's Taste

Try tasting a seasonal edible from nature—like a berry, a wild herb, or even a freshly picked fruit or vegetable straight from the garden. Savour the flavours mindfully, noticing how nature's bounty engages your palate and awakens your awareness.

 *Outcomes*
- Enhances sensory awareness by engaging your taste, smell, and touch.
- Cultivates mindfulness through the savouring of natural flavours.

 *Items*
A safe, edible seasonal item from nature (such as a wild berry, fresh herb, or bush-picked fruit/vegetable)

Intention: "I savour the gifts of the earth, appreciating the nourishment that nature provides."

 *Steps*

Find a quiet place in nature where you can sit peacefully— where you've come across something seasonal and edible that you know is safe to eat. It might be a freshly picked berry, a sprig of native herb, or a fruit still warm from the sun. Hold it in your hand for a moment. Take in its colour, its shape, its scent. Notice the way it feels—smooth, fuzzy, cool, or fragrant. Let your senses fully arrive before you even take a bite.

When you're ready, take a small taste. Don't rush. Let the flavours unfold slowly on your tongue. Is it sweet, tart, earthy, refreshing? Feel the texture as you chew, paying attention to every nuance, like a quiet conversation between your senses and the land.

As you eat, let yourself feel the life force within this food. It came from the earth, nourished by sun, rain, and soil—and now it's nourishing you. This is nature's energy, still humming with aliveness, now becoming part of your own.

Continue tasting mindfully for a few moments more, fully present with the experience. Let this small act of eating become something sacred—a moment of gratitude, of grounding, of deep connection with the land that provides. When you're done, sit quietly for a few breaths and thank the earth for its quiet, generous offering.

 *Reflect*
How did focusing on the flavours and textures enhance your overall experience?
What sensations or memories were evoked by the natural taste?

 *More*
Consider journalling your experience by describing the flavours, textures, and sensations.

Wind's Caress

The wind is a messenger, always moving, shifting, and touching everything in its path. In this practice, you allow yourself to fully experience the presence of the wind, tuning into its textures, temperatures, and movement —always in motion, always changing.

 *Outcomes*

- Cultivates mindfulness by bringing awareness to the sensations of wind.
- Encourages presence and openness to the natural elements.

 *Items*

An open space where you can feel the wind

Intention: "I allow the wind to touch my skin, reminding me that even the unseen can be deeply felt."

 *Steps*

Find an open spot outdoors where the wind moves freely—maybe a hilltop, a wide field, or a breezy garden clearing. Stand still for a moment and let your body settle into the space. Close your eyes or soften your gaze, and take a few slow, grounding breaths. Begin to notice the wind's first gentle touch on your skin. Is it cool or warm? Light as a whisper or playful and strong? Let yourself simply receive it, as if the wind is greeting you.

Tune into the movement—how does it shift and swirl around you? You might feel it brushing past your arms, tugging at your hair, or dancing across your cheeks. Let the sensations deepen your awareness of your own body in space—alive, present, and porous to the elements.

Now breathe with the wind. Inhale slowly, imagining you're drawing the air through your skin, into your lungs. Exhale just as gently, letting your breath blend with the breeze. You are part of the movement now—no separation, just flow.

Stand still and let the wind speak to you in its own language. It doesn't need words. Just feel. Maybe it brings clarity, lightness, energy—or maybe it simply reminds you that you're alive. When you're ready, bring a hand to your heart and take one last breath with the wind. Offer a silent thank you for its presence.

Reflect

How did it feel to focus solely on the wind's touch? What emotions or thoughts arose as you stood in stillness?

More

Try this practice in different types of wind—on a breezy morning, during a gentle dusk, or when the air is still.

Acoustic Meditation

Nature is filled with sounds—some subtle, some vibrant—all part of an ever-changing symphony. In this practice, you refine your listening by focusing on a single sound, using it as an anchor to presence. This practice invites you to attune fully to the moment.

 *Outcomes*
- Cultivates deep listening and heightened sensory awareness.
- Encourages mindfulness by focusing on a single point of attention.

 *Items*
A outdoor space where natural sounds are present.

Intention: "I close my eyes and listen, allowing sound to guide me into deep presence and stillness."

 *Steps*

Find a peaceful spot outdoors—maybe under the canopy of trees, beside a stream, or in the stillness of an open field. Sit comfortably and take a few slow, grounding breaths. Let your awareness gently open, taking in the full soundscape around you. Hear the rustle of leaves, the call of birds, the buzz of insects, maybe even the hush of your own breath.

Now, let one sound catch your attention. It might be the steady flow of water, a single bird's song, or the soft sigh of wind through branches. Let your focus gently rest there, as if you're tuning in to a story told just for you.

Notice everything about the sound—its tone, rhythm, the spaces between. Does it rise and fall? Does it stay steady or change with time? Let it become your anchor, guiding you deeper into stillness. There's nothing to figure out or analyse—just be with the sound. Let it hold you in the present moment, a thread connecting your inner world with the living land around you.

If your mind wanders, just notice and gently bring it back to the sound.

After a few minutes, take a deep breath. Open your ears once more to the full chorus of nature, noticing how rich and alive it feels. Carry this sense of quiet listening with you—a reminder that even a single sound can lead you home to yourself.

 *Reflect*
What did you notice about the sound when you focused solely on it? How did this practice shift your sense of presence?

 *More*
Try this meditation at different times of day or in different locations.

A Moment of Reflection

Before stepping into the next chapter, take a moment to reflect on your journey of sensing the world more fully.

Which of your senses felt most alive during these practices? Were you naturally drawn to touch, sound, scent, or another sense?
_____
_____
_____

How did engaging your senses shift your experience of nature? Did you notice details you may have overlooked before?
_____
_____
_____

Did any sense awaken a memory or deep emotion? What feelings or personal insights arose as you explored nature through sensory awareness?
_____
_____
_____

Did any practice feel uncomfortable or challenging? What happened when you allowed yourself to lean into the experience?
_____
_____
_____

Do you feel ready to move forward? The next chapter invites you to explore your creativity—expressing the beauty, sensations, and emotions you've discovered through nature-based art and playful exploration. Does this feel like a natural next step?

Take your time. Savour the journey. Let nature continue to reveal itself through every breath, touch, and whisper.

Chapter 5:
Create with the Land

Let the earth be your canvas,
a quiet, living tapestry where every ridge and root tells a story.
In the whisper of wind through golden grasses
and the gentle murmur of a distant stream,
find your muse.

Trace the contours of ancient hills
with the soft brushstrokes of your heart,
each moment unfolding like a vibrant blossom
under the tender care of nature.

In this sacred dance with the land,
you are both creator and creation—
a living echo of earth's timeless wonder.

Creating with the Land: Expression Through Connection

With presence, breath, heart, and the senses now awakened, you've begun to experience nature not just as something outside of you—but as something alive within you. The practices so far have deepened your ability to be with the land, to feel its rhythms, to receive its quiet offerings. Now, you are invited to *respond*. To enter into a dialogue with nature through your own creativity, curiosity, and expression.

This chapter is about *creating with the land*—not to change it, control it, or impress anyone—but as a way of honouring the relationship you're building with it. Just like a conversation between two dear friends, creative expression allows you to reflect, to play, to speak your inner experience in a way words often cannot.

This isn't about being "good" at art. It's about being present, being playful, and letting the land co-create with you. A line drawn in the dirt, a pattern made from fallen petals, a sculpture built with sticks—each is a reflection of your state of mind, your presence, your willingness to engage.

Creating with Nature in Ancient Wisdom

Since the beginning of time, humans have expressed themselves through nature. Long before paintbrushes or canvas, art was made with the land itself—drawn into earth, carved into stone, woven from grasses, and dyed with plant pigments. In many ancient cultures, these acts of creation were not considered "art" as we define it today, but sacred offerings—ways of communicating with the divine, with ancestors, and with the natural world.

In Indigenous Australian cultures, expression through ochre painting, sand drawings, carvings, and songlines connects people to Country, story, and spirit. These are not random marks—they are living maps of land, identity, ancestry, and belonging. Every symbol, every gesture holds deep meaning, carried through generations. To create with nature is to honour the land and one's place within it.

In Celtic traditions, natural materials like willow, stone, feathers, and fire were used in ritual and seasonal celebration. Crafting was a way of aligning with the cycles of the earth—honouring solstices, equinoxes, and the sacredness of the seasons.

In Hindu and Buddhist traditions, mandalas are created with coloured sand, flowers, or grains—meticulously placed in patterns that reflect the harmony of the cosmos. And when complete, they are gently swept away, a reminder of life's impermanence and the beauty of letting go.

These traditions remind us that creating with nature is not about permanence or performance—it is about *presence*. About using what is already offered by the land, with respect and reverence.

Art as Pathways to Deep Connection

Creating with nature is not just about making something—it's about *feeling something*. It's about entering into a state of flow where the boundaries between self and world begin to dissolve. When we make art with the earth—when we gather leaves, trace shapes in sand, arrange petals, or carve patterns into bark with our fingertips—we are slowing down enough to listen, to notice, and to *respond*.

In this space of creativity, we're not trying to fix, produce, or impress. We are simply expressing what's inside of us in harmony with what surrounds us. The materials of the land hold texture, energy, and memory. When we create with them, we are entering a kind of relationship—a quiet exchange that doesn't need words.

This act of making becomes a bridge between the inner and outer world. It helps us process emotion, release tension, and access joy and imagination. Even more, it deepens our *attention*. As we study the lines of a leaf, notice the exact hue of a flower, or shape a sculpture from river stones, we are drawn into intimacy with nature. It is this attention—this care—that turns a simple act into something sacred.

You might be surprised how healing it feels to create freely and gently, without judgment. The beauty is in the process, not the product. The meaning is in the moment, not the outcome. Art made with the land reminds us that we, too, are creative beings—fluid, expressive, part of nature's great unfolding.

Let this chapter be a celebration of that. A return to play, to presence, to possibility. Let your hands be curious. Let your heart lead the way. And trust that whatever you create, no matter how simple, is part of something much greater—a quiet act of connection that leaves both you and the land a little more whole.

As you engage with the practices in this chapter, know that you are stepping into an ancient rhythm—one where expression is natural, intuitive, and deeply connected to the earth. Let the land guide your hands. Let your creations be gifts, not for display, but for the joy of the moment and the quiet exchange between you and the wild.

Mindful Rock Painting

Express reflections through painting on natural surfaces. This mindful art activity encourages self-reflection and emotional awareness by choosing a rock that resonates with you and painting it with a word, symbol, or pattern that represents your current feelings.

- Encourages self-expression and emotional reflection.
- Develops mindfulness by focusing on the present moment.

Smooth rocks, Paint or paint pens
Brushes and water (if using paint)

Intention: "I bring presence and intention, creating in harmony with the earth."

Head outside to a place where you feel relaxed and unhurried—somewhere the land invites you to pause. Take a few deep breaths to centre yourself and soften into the moment. Let your eyes wander the ground until you find a rock that calls to you—not the perfect one, but the one that feels just right in your hand. Maybe it's smooth and cool, maybe rough and weathered. Trust your instinct.

Sit down with your chosen rock and simply hold it. Let its weight ground you. When you're ready, take out some paint, chalk, or markers and begin to decorate the rock. You might draw a symbol, write a word, or simply create shapes and colours that match your mood. There's no right way to do this—just let your feelings move through your hands and onto the stone. Let it be your little portrait of this moment in time.

As you work, notice what it feels like to express something without words. There's no pressure for it to be perfect—this is about connection, not art class.

Once your rock is dry, you might choose to keep it somewhere meaningful, as a reminder of what you felt and expressed. Or, when you're ready, return it to the earth—placing it gently in a special spot, like a quiet offering of your inner world to the land that held you. Either way, your expression has found its way into form, into nature, and into your story.

Why did you choose this specific rock?
How did the process of painting help you express your emotions?

Create a "Gratitude Rock Garden" where each rock represents something you're thankful for.

Leaf Breathing Art

Combine nature, creativity, and breath awareness in a calming art practice. This activity encourages a deep connection between breath and creativity by using leaves as inspiration for artistic expression.

 *Outcomes*
- Develops mindfulness through breath awareness while creating art.
- Encourages focus and patience in detailed artistic work.

 *Items*
Leaves of different shapes and sizes, Paper or a journal Pencils, fine-tip markers, or watercolour paints & brushes

Intention: "I use my breath to create allowing the leaves to remind me of life's gentle rhythm."

 *Steps*

Find a quiet place outdoors or by a sunny window—with a leaf that you're drawn to. Take a moment to sit with it. Hold it in your hand and breathe deeply—in and out—allowing yourself to arrive in this moment. Look closely at the leaf. Trace its edges with your eyes, notice the veins that stretch like tiny rivers across its surface. Feel its texture, its temperature, its stillness. Let your breath move slowly, in rhythm with your observing.

Now place the leaf on a piece of paper and trace its shape, or simply paint a soft outline of it. Don't rush. Let your hand follow the lines with care.

As you begin to fill the inside of the leaf with lines, patterns, or gentle shapes, match each mark to your breath. Inhale… draw a curve. Exhale… add a swirl. Let the breath guide your art, so that each stroke becomes a reflection of your inner rhythm.

There's no need to plan or perfect—this is about the process, not the product. Allow your designs to unfold naturally, just like the leaf once did. With each breath, you're creating a quiet expression of presence, beauty, and connection.

When your leaf is full, pause. Take a step back and look at what you've created. It's more than just a drawing—it's a breath-made meditation, a moment of stillness made visible. Let it remind you of the gentle harmony between you and the natural world.

 *Reflect*

How did focusing on your breath change the way you created your art? Did you notice any patterns in nature that inspired your designs?

 *More*

Create a series of breath-inspired leaf designs and arrange them into a "mindful forest" collage.

Sky Doodling

Observe the sky's ever-changing canvas and express your impressions through art. This mindful art activity encourages you to slow down, observe the sky, and creatively interpret cloud shapes and movement.

 **Outcomes**
- Develops observation skills by studying cloud formations.
- Encourages mindfulness through present-moment awareness.

 **Items**
Sketchbook or journal
Pastels, watercolours, or coloured pencils

Intention: "I let my imagination wander, creating from a place of lightness and play."

 **Steps**

Find a quiet outdoor space where you can lie down and see the open sky. Let your body settle and take a few slow, deep breaths. With each exhale, allow yourself to sink a little more into the earth beneath you. Turn your attention to the sky above. Watch how the clouds drift and dance, how the colours shift—soft blues, glowing whites, maybe even shades of grey or gold. Let your imagination wander. Do the shapes remind you of anything? There's no need to rush—just be with the sky and whatever it stirs in you.

When you feel inspired, reach for your journal or art supplies and begin to draw. Maybe you sketch exactly what you see. Or maybe you let your emotions and impressions guide you, turning the sky into an abstract story of the moment. Use colours, textures, or simple lines—whatever flows.

If words arise, follow them. You might write a short reflection, a poem, or even just a single phrase that captures the feeling this sky gives you. Let the sky be your muse—shifting, fleeting, full of emotion.

Before you pack away your things, pause for a moment and simply look up once more. Let your heart fill with appreciation for the ever-changing sky—an artist in its own right, and now part of your own expression too.

 **Reflect**
What emotions did the sky evoke for you today?
Did you see any recognisable shapes or patterns?

 **More**
Create a cloud-watching journal to record sky observations over time.

Shadow Drawing

Observe and trace the ever-changing dance of shadows in nature. This activity encourages mindfulness and an appreciation for time's passage by observing and tracing the movement of tree shadows.

- Develops observation skills and time awareness through shadow movement.
- Enhances artistic expression by tracing and layering natural shapes.

Large sheets of paper or a sketchbook
Pencils, charcoal, or fine-tip markers

Intention: "I trace the shifting dance of light and shadow, embracing impermanence in my art."

Find a spot outdoors where light and shadow play together—under a tree, near a cluster of leaves, or even beside a tall wildflower. Let the sun cast its patterns clearly onto the ground, and when you find a shadow that intrigues you, place your paper beside it.

Take a moment to breathe and settle, then begin lightly tracing the shape the shadow makes. Follow its curves or angles with gentle focus, letting your hand move slowly. This is your first layer—a moment in time, captured in light and shade.

Come back to this same spot later in the day—maybe in the afternoon, or again the next morning. Notice how the shadows have shifted. Trace them again, layering the new lines over the old. With each return, you're recording not just the movement of the sun, but the passage of time itself. As your drawing becomes more layered, more alive, you might choose to add shading, colours, or patterns to show the changes. Let the page become a dance of shifting light—a quiet collaboration between you and the sun.

There's no right or wrong way to finish. Let your piece evolve naturally. And when you're done, pause to reflect on what it felt like to return to the same spot, to witness change, and to create alongside nature's own rhythm. In a way, this is not just shadow drawing—it's time drawing. And you were part of it.

How did the shadows change throughout the day?
What did you notice about the relationship between light, and time?

Use this technique to create a time-lapse artwork by repeating the activity over multiple days or seasons.

Nature Rubbings

Discover the hidden textures of nature and reflect on their meaning. This activity encourages mindful observation and creativity. By pairing the art with reflective writing you develop a deeper connection to your surroundings and emotions.

 *Outcomes*
- Enhances observation skills by exploring textures in nature.
- Encourages self-expression through both visual art and written reflection.

 *Items*
Paper, Crayons, pencils or charcoal, A journal or notebook
A variety of natural surfaces (tree bark, leaves, stones)

Intention: "I uncover the hidden textures of the land."

 *Steps*

Head out for a slow wander through nature with open eyes and curious hands. As you move, begin to notice the different textures around you. When something catches your attention, pause. Hold a piece of paper over the surface and gently rub over it with a crayon or some charcoal. Watch as the hidden patterns begin to emerge—like nature's fingerprint revealed on your page. Take your time. Let your movements be slow and mindful.

Collect a few different rubbings as you walk—choosing a variety of textures, from rough to smooth, bumpy to soft. Each one holds a different story. Once you've gathered several, find a quiet place to sit. Lay your rubbings out in front of you and take a moment to really look at them. How does each texture make you feel? What do they remind you of? Is there one that feels calming, another that feels bold or wild?

Let your reflections spill onto the page—perhaps as a short piece of writing, a stream of thoughts, or even a poem inspired by the feel and form of what you touched. Let the textures guide your words, just as they guided your hands.

In this practice, you're not just making art—you're letting the land speak through texture, through feeling, through story. And in doing so, you're weaving yourself a little more closely into the fabric of the natural world.

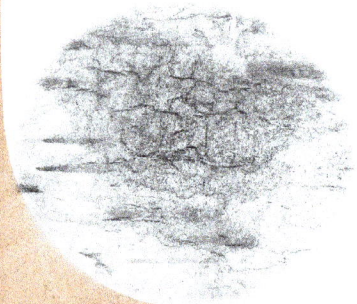

 *Reflect*
What textures surprised you the most?
How did different surfaces make you feel?

 *More*
Create a "texture map" of a favourite outdoor space by collecting rubbings from different locations and writing a story or poem that connects them.

Soundscape Sketching

Transform outdoor sounds into visual art through mindful listening and abstract drawing. This activity encourages deep listening and creative interpretation by transforming sounds into shapes, patterns, and lines.

- Enhances auditory awareness and deep listening skills.
- Encourages creative self-expression through abstract art.

Sketchbook or paper.
Pencils, charcoal, or pastels.

Intention: "I allow the sounds of nature to translate their rhythm into lines, shapes, and movement."

Find a quiet spot in nature where you can sit undisturbed. Let the space invite you into stillness. Sit down, take a few deep breaths, and close your eyes for a moment. Begin to listen—not just hearing, but really tuning in. Notice the layers of sound around you: birds calling in bursts or wind weaving through leaves. Let each sound arrive as it is, without labelling or needing to understand.

Now open your eyes slowly and pick up your sketchbook or a blank page. With your pencil or pen, begin to translate what you hear into lines, shapes, and patterns. There's no need to draw the source of the sound—this isn't about recreating what you see. Instead, let your marks be a kind of visual music.

You might draw sharp, jagged lines to match a high-pitched birdcall. Or soft, rolling curves to reflect the breeze. Maybe dots for the pitter-patter of raindrops, or swirls for distant echoes. Let your hand move in response to what your ears are experiencing.

Keep sketching as long as the sounds keep flowing. Let the landscape move through you, from ear to hand to page. When you're ready to finish, pause and take in your drawing. It's a map of your moment—a visual memory of how it felt to listen deeply to the world around you. Let it remind you how closely sound and creativity—and you—are woven into the rhythm of the land.

Which sounds stood out to you the most?
How did different sounds influence the marks you made?

Repeat this activity in different environments (forest, beach, city park) and compare how the soundscapes influence your sketches.

Calming Petals

Draw or paint flowers with large petals, then use each petal to write or illustrate something calming. This creative exercise invites you to slow down and connect with your inner sense of peace, using the flower as a canvas for mindfulness and self-expression.

 *Outcomes*
- Enhances your mindfulness by linking creative expression with calming thoughts.
- Encourages emotional reflection and self-soothing through art.

 *Items*
Paper or a journal
Pencils, watercolours, or pastels

Intention: "I invite each petal to teach me about peace, love, and quiet joy."

 *Steps*

Find a quiet spot in nature—or even near a window with a view of the outdoors—where you feel inspired to create. Let it be a place where the air feels gentle and your mind can soften. Bring your art materials and settle in, allowing yourself to arrive slowly with a few deep breaths.

Begin by drawing or painting a large flower on your page. Let the shape emerge naturally—round and full, or wild and whimsical. Focus on the beauty of the petals as you create them, one by one, as if the flower is slowly blooming from the centre outwards.

Now, with each petal you add, take a moment to pause and reflect. What brings you a sense of calm? It might be a single word like "stillness," a symbol like a wave or a moon, or even a tiny sketch—your bare feet on warm grass, the hug of a loved one, the quiet of dusk. Add that word or image inside the petal. Let each one hold a small expression of peace.

Let the process be slow and intuitive. There's no rush, no rules. Just a simple practice of beauty and presence, one petal at a time.

When your flower is complete, take a moment to sit with it. Notice how each petal, each thought, each breath of calm comes together to form something whole and radiant—like you. Let your Breathing Blossom be a reminder that peace is made up of many small, quiet things, and they're all already within you.

 *Reflect*
How did focusing on each petal influence your mood and awareness? What emotions or thoughts emerged as you added calming details to your flower?

More
Try this practice using different flowers or natural elements, exploring how various forms influence your state of mind.

Texture Sketch

Gently trace natural objects (leaves, bark, flowers) with your fingers before sketching their shapes and textures. Fully engage your sense of touch and become more attuned to the details of nature before translating them into a drawing.

- Enhances your sensory awareness and mindfulness through tactile exploration.
- Encourages creative observation by linking touch with visual expression.

A selection of natural objects
Paper, A pencil, pen, or any drawing implement

Intention: "I explore the landscape through touch, allowing myself to connect with the the earth."

As you walk through nature, let your eyes land on something that draws you in—a fallen leaf with intricate veins, a curled piece of bark, a stone worn smooth by time. Hold the object in your hand. Close your eyes and begin to slowly trace its edges and surface with your fingers. Explore its curves, its bumps, the softness or sharpness of its texture. Let your sense of touch guide you into the object's story—where it's been, how it's grown.

After a few moments, place the object beside you and take out your drawing materials. Begin sketching—not just what you see, but what you felt. Let your hands remember the shapes, the ridges, the subtle shifts in surface. Translate those sensations into lines and shadows, into gentle impressions on the page.

There's no need to make it perfect. This isn't about getting it "right"—it's about presence, about turning touch into art. Let the drawing unfold slowly and naturally, one mark at a time.

As you finish, sit with both your drawing and the object. Notice how your awareness has deepened—how something small and quiet can invite you into stillness, into detail, into connection with the land and with yourself.

How did tracing the object with your fingers change the way you perceived its texture?
What new details did you notice through touch that you might have overlooked by just looking?

Try tracing and drawing several different objects in one sitting to compare how each one engages your senses.

One-Line Drawing

Choose an object and draw it using one continuous line, staying fully present in the process. This exercise emphasises the journey of expression over the end result, encouraging you to embrace imperfection and trust your instincts.

- Enhances your focus and mindfulness.
- Encourages you to let go of perfection and immerse yourself in the present moment.

A natural object (such as a leaf, flower, stone, or branch) that catches your eye

Intention: "I trust the flow of my hand, letting nature's energy move through me as I create."

Wander slowly until you find a natural object that speaks to you. Choose something with shape and character, something that makes you want to look a little closer. Bring it with you to a quiet place where you can sit comfortably. Place it in front of you, and take a few slow, grounding breaths. Let your gaze soften as you begin to really observe the object. Notice its curves, its edges, its tiny imperfections.

Now, pick up your pencil or pen, and place it on your paper. Here's the invitation: without lifting your drawing tool, begin to draw the object using just one continuous line. Let your hand move slowly and steadily, tracing what you see in a single breath of movement.

Stay fully present. Don't worry if the lines wobble or overlap—this isn't about perfection. It's about staying connected, letting your hand and eye move together in quiet attention.

When you reach the end, gently lift your pencil. Take a moment to look at what you've created. Notice how the lines capture the spirit of the object—not in detail, but in flow, in feeling, in presence.

Let the drawing be a reflection of how it felt to slow down, to see with care, and to let go of control. Sometimes, the simplest lines tell the truest stories.

How did focusing on one continuous line affect your connection with the object?
What sensations did you notice in your body and mind as you allowed your hand to flow freely?

Try this practice with different objects.

Sunset Silhouette

Watch the sunset and paint its colours and shapes focusing on the transition of light and the emotions it brings. Allow yourself to be fully present, absorbing the beauty of the natural light and the emotions it evokes as you connect with the fleeting beauty of the evening.

- Enhances mindfulness by drawing your attention to natural transitions
- Cultivates your inner expression and observation skills.

Paper or canvas, Paints (watercolours, acrylics, or oils)
Paintbrushes and water
View of the sunset

Intention: "I pause to honour the closing of the day, capturing the golden hour with appreciation."

 Find a peaceful place where you can watch the sunset unfold. Settle in and take a few deep, steady breaths. Let your body soften, and allow the day to begin its gentle closing. As the sun begins to dip, turn your full attention to the sky. Notice how the colours shift slowly—bright golds fading to soft pinks and deep purples. Watch the silhouettes begin to form—trees, rooftops, distant hills—turning darker as the light fades behind them.

With your paper in front of you, begin by sketching the main shapes you see. Keep it loose and simple—just the outline of the land and sky. As the colours deepen, start layering in paint or pastels, following the light's lead. Let your brush or fingers move in time with the slow dance of dusk.

Allow your emotions to guide you. Maybe the sunset brings a sense of peace, or wonder, or even a quiet kind of longing. Let that feeling find its way into your work—not through exact detail, but through tone, movement, colour, and flow. There's no rush. The sunset itself moves slowly. Follow its rhythm until the sky begins to darken and the moment feels complete.

When you're done, sit for a few more breaths with your painting and the fading light. What you've created is more than just a picture—it's a memory of presence, a reflection of how the land and light moved through you in one soft, beautiful moment.

 *How did the changing colours and shadows of the sunset affect your mood and sense of presence?*
What emotions arose as you observed the interplay of light and dark?

 Take a few moments to journal about your experience and the emotions the sunset evoked.

Stillness Silhouettes

Observe, slow down, and capture the essence of nature through shape. This activity encourages mindfulness and focused observation by drawing only the silhouette of an object, animal, or tree.

- Develops focus and patience through still observation.
- Enhances the ability to see shapes and forms without distraction.

Sketchbook or paper, Pencil, charcoal, or black marker

Intention: "I trace the outlines of nature's stillness, finding my own sense of calm in the process."

Find a peaceful place outdoors where you can sit quietly and observe without interruption. Take a few deep, slow breaths and allow your body to settle, softening into stillness. Let your eyes gently explore the space around you until something catches your attention—a tree standing tall, a bird perched on a branch, or even a uniquely shaped rock.

This isn't about analysing the details. Just take in the outer shape. Let your focus rest on the outline—the curves, the angles, the way it meets the sky or the ground. As you breathe, let your awareness stay with that outer form, like you're seeing it for the first time.

With a pencil or marker in hand, begin to draw the silhouette. Follow the edge of the shape slowly, without rushing. Don't worry about perfection—this is a practice in presence, not precision. You might decide to fill in the silhouette completely, colouring it dark, or you might leave it as a simple outline.

When your drawing feels complete, look back at the subject in front of you. Compare your simple shape with the real thing—noticing how the essence of what you observed is captured, even without the details. Let this be a reminder that sometimes the outer shape holds just as much beauty as what lies within.

What did you notice about your subject that you might not have seen before?
How did it feel to focus only on shape rather than details?

Try this activity at different times of day to explore how lighting and shadows affect silhouettes.

Dew Drop Drawing

Capture the delicate beauty of morning dew through art and observation. Embrace the quiet of early morning by observing and sketching dew drops on grass, or spiderwebs. Through careful attention to detail develop patience, focus, and an appreciation for nature.

 **Outcomes**
- Enhances close observation skills and appreciation for natural patterns.
- Encourages mindfulness by focusing on small, fleeting details in nature.

 **Items**
Sketchbook or paper
Pencil, fine-tip pen, or watercolour paints

Intention: "I create with the most fleeting of canvases, embracing the beauty of the present moment."

 **Steps**

Rise early and step gently into the hush of the morning, when the world is still wrapped in softness. Head outside to a place where the grass grows wild, leaves hang low, or spiderwebs stretch between branches. Let your eyes search for the tiny jewels of the dawn—drops of dew clinging delicately to every surface.

Take your time to really look. Notice how the droplets catch the light, how they reflect the world in miniature. Some gather in perfect spheres, while others stretch and shimmer like tiny lanterns. Settle into the moment and begin to sketch what you see. Let your pencil or pen trace the curves and shine of each droplet. Play with shading—soft, rounded shadows—and gentle highlights to capture the glisten.

As you draw, stay connected to the quiet around you. Notice how the coolness of the air, the stillness of the land, and the presence of dew affect your mood. Does it feel peaceful? Precious? Does it bring up memories or stir something new?

There's something sacred about these early hours—when everything feels fresh and alive, and beauty reveals itself in the smallest details. Let this practice be a reminder that even a single drop of water can hold the light of the whole morning.

 **Reflect**
What did you notice about the way dew forms and clings to surfaces? How does light change the appearance of the droplets?

 **More**
Try drawing dew drops at different times of the morning to see how they change as the sun rises.

Sit Spot Sketching

Tune into nature's essence and translate its feeling into art. This activity encourages quiet observation with nature. Instead of drawing specific objects, focus on capturing the overall mood, energy, and feeling of the space through colour, texture, and abstract forms.

 *Outcomes*
- Encourages mindfulness by fostering deep observation and presence.
- Enhances emotional expression through abstract or impressionistic art.

 *Items*
Sketchbook or watercolour paper, pencil, charcoal, pastels, or watercolours

Intention: "I let my surroundings inspire me, capturing what I see, feel, and sense."

 *Steps*

Find a quiet place in nature that feels just right—somewhere you can sit undisturbed for a little while. Settle in and take a few deep breaths, letting your body soften into stillness. For the next five minutes or so, simply be here. No need to do anything yet—just observe. Let your senses open wide. Feel the air moving across your skin. Notice the light—how it filters through leaves or reflects off a surface. Listen to the layers of sound. Notice how being in this place makes you feel.

When you're ready, pick up your sketchbook or paints. But instead of drawing the trees or birds around you, begin to express how the space feels. Use colours, shapes, and textures to capture the mood of this moment. Is it soft and slow? Bright and alive? Still and deep?

Let your hand move with intuition. There's no right or wrong way to do this. You might find yourself swirling colour like the wind, layering soft tones like filtered light, or using jagged strokes to mirror a sense of movement. Follow your feeling more than your thinking.

This isn't a picture of what you see—it's a reflection of how this place is meeting you today. When you pause and look at your artwork, you might see not just nature, but yourself in it too—quietly connected, and gently expressed.

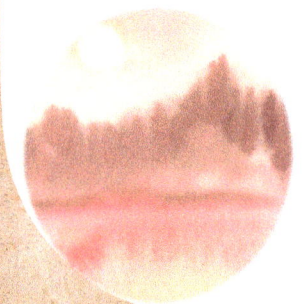

 *Reflect*
What emotions or sensations did this space bring up for you? How did it feel to capture an experience rather than a specific object?

 *More*
Return to the same sit spot at different times of day or in different weather conditions.

Tactile Clay Creations

Engage the senses by sculpting with touch rather than sight. By removing visual input, you heighten their sensory awareness, fostering mindfulness and a deeper connection to texture, shape, and movement.

 *Outcomes*
- Enhances sensory awareness by focusing on touch rather than sight.
- Encourages mindfulness through slow, intentional movements.

 *Items*
A small ball of clay or soft natural earth

Intention: "I shape and mould, letting nature's textures awaken creativity within me."

 *Steps*

Find a calm space where you can sit undisturbed—outdoors if possible. Bring a small piece of clay or natural earth, and settle into a comfortable seat. Take a few slow breaths and allow your body to soften into the moment. Close your eyes, or gently tie a blindfold if that feels comfortable. With your sight turned inward, bring your awareness to your hands. Pick up the clay and begin to knead it slowly. Notice its texture—is it smooth or gritty? Cool or warm? Sticky or soft? Let your fingers explore without any plan, just feeling.

Begin shaping the clay into whatever wants to emerge. Don't try to control it—just follow the gentle movement of your hands. Maybe it becomes a spiral, a bowl, a creature, or something completely abstract. This is a creation born of touch, not vision.

Stay with the process for as long as it feels grounding and good. Let the clay guide you—pressing, smoothing, shaping—with no pressure to make anything in particular. When you feel finished, slowly open your eyes. Look at what you've created. What does it remind you of? What feelings or memories does it stir?

Let your creation be a reminder that beauty and expression live in all your senses—and that sometimes, closing your eyes allows your inner world to come into clearer view.

 *Reflect*
How did sculpting with closed eyes change your experience of working with clay?
What textures or sensations stood out to you the most?

 *More*
Try this activity again using different materials, such as wet sand, soft leaves, or even tree bark.

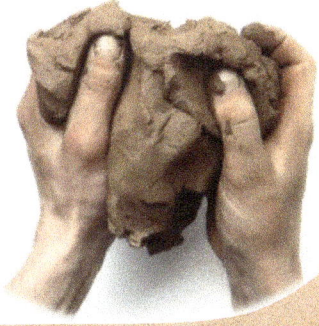

Cloud Shape Creations

Turn drifting clouds into imaginative creations. By watching the ever-changing sky, you practice mindfulness, creativity, and playfulness while strengthening your ability to see possibilities in abstract shapes.

- Develops observational skills and creativity by interpreting cloud shapes.
- Encourages mindfulness by fostering present-moment awareness.

A sketchbook or piece of paper
Pencils, coloured pencils, or pastels

Intention: "I let my imagination drift with the sky, turning clouds into stories and dreams."

Find a peaceful place outdoors where you can lie back or sit comfortably with a clear view of the sky. Take a few deep, calming breaths and allow your gaze to lift upward. Begin to observe the clouds drifting above you. Notice their shapes, sizes, and how they move. Some may be wispy and fast, others slow and billowing. Watch them change, expand, dissolve.

When one catches your attention, quickly sketch its shape—just the outline. Don't worry about getting it perfect—the clouds are changing as you draw, and that's part of the magic. Now use your imagination to transform that shape into something new. Maybe you see a sleeping dragon, a dancing jellyfish, or a floating island. Add little details—eyes, wings, patterns, or landscapes—until the cloud becomes something entirely your own.

Keep going if you'd like. Choose new clouds and create a collection of transformations. Let your drawings flow freely and playfully, guided by what you see and what your inner world wants to express.

When you're done, take a moment to sit with your sky-born creations. What surprised you? Was it the shapes the clouds took on—or what your mind made of them? Let this be a reminder of how alive your imagination is, and how even the passing sky can become a canvas for creativity.

What did you first notice about the clouds?
How did it feel to watch the clouds shift and change?

Try turning your cloud drawings into a short story, poem, or comic strip.

Puddle Painting

Look into a puddle and sketch or paint what you see. Notice how the light creates shimmering reflections, how ripples distort the image, and the fleeting beauty of the moment. Capture these details allowing the ephemeral qualities of water to inspire you.

 *Outcomes*
- Enhances your sensory awareness by focusing on the subtle interplay of light
- Encourages mindfulness and deep observation as you translate nature's beauty into art.

 *Items*
A puddle
Paper or canvas
Pencils, watercolours, pastels

Intention: "I play with reflection and movement, letting water teach me about fluidity and change."

 *Steps*

Find a small puddle in nature—perhaps after rain, Make sure it's safe to sit or stand nearby, where you can see its surface clearly. Settle in, and take a few slow, grounding breaths to arrive fully in the moment. Begin by simply observing. Let your eyes soften as you watch the surface of the water. Notice how the light dances across it, how tiny ripples come and go, how reflections shimmer—trees, sky, clouds, maybe even your own outline.

Take your time with this quiet witnessing. There's no need to rush. This is about seeing, really seeing—how the puddle is more than just a patch of water, but a small mirror of the world and its ever-shifting beauty. When you feel ready, begin sketching or painting what you see. Let your hand follow the movement of the reflections, the swirl of colour, the shape of a ripple. You don't need to capture everything perfectly—just respond to what's there. Be guided by the fluidity of the moment.

Let your creative process unfold gently. The puddle may change as the light shifts or as wind stirs the surface. That's part of the magic. You're painting something that is always in motion—always becoming. When your artwork feels complete, sit quietly for a moment. Reflect on the experience of creating with something so fleeting, so delicate.

 *Reflect*

How did observing the delicate details of the puddle affect your sense of presence?
Which aspects of the reflections, ripples, or light stood out to you, and why?

 *More*

Return to the same puddle at different times of day to notice how the changing light transforms its appearance.

Wishing Stones

Paint smooth stones with wishes, hopes, or affirmations. Once decorated, return them to nature as a gentle, mindful offering, symbolising your desire to share positivity and connect with the world around you.

 **Outcomes**
- Enhances mindfulness by linking creative expression with heartfelt intentions.
- Encourages emotional reflection and self-affirmation through decorating the stones.

 **Items**
A selection of smooth stones
Paints, paintbrushes, or markers

Intention: "I hold my stone with intention, placing my hopes within it."

 **Steps**

Take a quiet wander through a natural space and gather a few smooth stones—ones that feel good in your hands. Find a peaceful place to sit, and take a few deep, grounding breaths to settle into the moment. Lay out your stones and your art supplies—paints, markers, or even natural dyes. Before you begin decorating, take a moment with each stone. What hope, wish, or affirmation is resting in your heart? A word like "peace" or "strength"? A simple symbol that holds meaning for you?

Begin to decorate your stones, letting your hand move slowly and intentionally. As you paint or draw, focus on the meaning behind each word or image. Let your creativity become a quiet form of reflection—each mark a way of speaking from the inside out.

When your stones are complete and the designs have dried, take a little walk. Find a spot in nature where you can leave each stone—a garden bed, beneath a favourite tree, tucked gently along a walking path. Place them with care, like small offerings of hope and connection. Before you leave, pause for a moment. Breathe. Feel the simple beauty of having expressed something true and placed it into the world.

 **Reflect**
How did the act of decorating each stone influence your mood or mindset?
What intentions or emotions emerged as you created your wishes and affirmations?

 **More**
Consider journalling about the experience, detailing the wishes or affirmations you chose.

Walking Doodles

Capture the beauty of the moment with mindful sketching on a slow nature walk. This activity encourages observation, creativity, and mindfulness by combining walking with spontaneous sketching.

 **Outcomes**
- Enhances observation skills and artistic expression.
- Develops mindfulness through focused sketching and present-moment awareness.

 **Items**
A small sketchbook, Pencil or fine-tip pen
Optional: coloured pencils or watercolours

Intention: "I let my steps guide my creativity.."

Steps

Head out for a slow, mindful walk through nature—whether it's a familiar path or a quiet corner of a nearby park. Let your breath guide your pace, soft and steady. Every few minutes, pause. Let your gaze wander until something catches your eye—a curled leaf, a single feather, the shifting pattern of clouds. Move a little closer. Notice the details. What shape does it take? What texture? How does it make you feel?

Now pull out your journal and sketch what you see. It doesn't have to be perfect—it's about presence, not polish. Let your hand move freely, capturing the essence of the moment in a few simple lines. Then keep walking. Pause again when something new calls to you. Repeat the process—observe, sketch, walk. Let the pages fill with little snapshots of what you encountered, a trail of doodles marking your journey.

When your walk comes to an end, take a moment to flip through your sketches. What stood out to you? How did it feel to slow down and draw in real time, surrounded by the life of the land? Let this be a reminder that art doesn't always need a studio—it can grow from the rhythm of your steps, the turn of your head, and the simple act of being awake to the world around you.

 **Reflect**
How did sketching affect the way you observed nature?
What small details did you notice that you might have overlooked?

 **More**
Turn your walking doodles into a nature journal by adding short written reflections, colours, or textures.

Echo Art

Translate the energy of nature into colours, lines, and patterns. This activity invites you to sit in stillness and tune into the atmosphere of your surroundings and create abstract art that visually "echoes" what you experience.

- Encourages deep listening and sensory awareness of nature's rhythms.
- Develops abstract artistic expression through intuitive mark-making.

Chalk, pastels, or coloured pencils
Large paper, sketchbook, or pavement (if using chalk)

Intention: "I create in response to what I see and hear, letting nature's voice shape my expression."

Find a peaceful place outdoors. Settle in and get comfortable. Close your eyes for a moment and take a few slow, grounding breaths. Begin to listen, really listen. Notice the layers of sound around you—the rustling of leaves, a distant bird call, the hum of insects, the whisper of wind across the grass. Let the sounds come and go without needing to name or label them. Just receive them.

When you feel ready, open your eyes and pick up your drawing tools. Begin making marks on the page—lines, shapes, colours, patterns—anything that captures what you're hearing and feeling. There's no need to make it look like something specific. This is your visual echo of the space. Let your hand move freely. A sharp bird call might become a zigzag. A soft breeze might appear as swirling lines. Let each sound guide the next movement of your pencil or brush.

As you continue, stay tuned into the space around you. Let the environment shift your artwork moment by moment. This is a collaboration between you and the land—a drawing made not from what you see, but from what you sense. When it feels complete, pause and look at your creation. Notice how it holds the energy of the place, the moment, and the quiet way you've been part of it. Let it remind you that art can come from anywhere—even the air.

What did you notice about the sounds and energy of the space?
How did translating these sensations into art make you feel?

Repeat this activity in different locations (a forest, beach, city park) and compare how each environment influences your artistic choices..

Fossil Imprint

Nature holds the stories of the past—imprinted in the rings of trees, the layers of rock, and the fossils left behind. In this practice, you create your own "fossils" by pressing natural objects into soft clay or earth, inviting you to consider the passage of time.

- Encourages mindful observation of patterns and textures in nature.
- Connects creativity with science by exploring how imprints preserve a moment in time.

Soft clay, mud, Leaves, shells, twigs, pinecones, or other textured natural objects

Intention: "I press into the earth, honouring the marks of time and the stories held within stone."

Find a soft surface in nature—damp sand, smooth clay, or a patch of soft mud. Take a slow breath and settle into the moment, letting your hands and eyes begin to explore. Look around and gather a few natural objects that catch your attention—maybe a leaf with deep veins, a shell with ridges, or a seedpod with an unusual shape. Take your time to really notice their details before you begin. Feel their texture, trace their contours, and imagine the stories they hold.

When you're ready, gently press one of your objects into the surface. Don't force it—just let it settle in and leave its mark. Slowly lift it away and observe the imprint left behind. What do you see? A delicate pattern? A fossil-like memory? Keep going, making more impressions if you like. Each one is a moment captured in texture—brief, beautiful, and unique. Let yourself imagine: What stories might this imprint tell if found years from now? What emotions or memories live within its shape?

If you're working with natural earth, you might choose to leave your creations as a quiet offering to the landscape—trusting the wind or rain to gently erase them, like time softening footprints. If you're using clay, set your imprint aside to dry, preserving it as a keepsake of this simple, earthy moment.

What did you notice about the details left behind in the imprints?
How does this practice remind you of the way time preserves or erases moments?

Create a series of imprints over time, documenting the changing textures of nature throughout the seasons.

A Moment of Reflection

Before stepping into the next chapter, take a moment to reflect on your journey of creativity and connection with nature.

How did it feel to create with nature rather than separate from it? Did you notice a difference in the way you approached creativity?

_____
_____
_____

What did you discover about yourself through these practices? Did any emotions, memories, or insights arise as you worked with natural materials?

_____
_____
_____

Did you notice a shift in how you see the land? Do you feel more attuned to the textures, colours, and shapes of the natural world around you?

_____
_____
_____

How did creating with nature affect your sense of presence? Did you find yourself more deeply engaged in the moment as you shaped, arranged, or painted with the earth's offerings?

_____
_____
_____

Do you feel ready to move forward? The next chapter invites you into the art of storytelling—giving voice to your experiences, emotions, and reflections. Does this feel like a natural next step?

Take your time. Let your creativity flow naturally, knowing that every mark, every moment, and every interaction with the land is part of a larger story waiting to be told.

Chapter 6:
Storytelling with Nature

*In the hush of a forest,
where leaves whisper secrets
and ancient trees keep silent diaries,
I find a language deeper than words—
a story written in the wind.*

*Every fallen leaf
carries a verse of lost summers,
each ring in the tree trunk
marks a chapter of endurance and change.
Nature sings in the rustle of grasses
and the gentle murmur of a hidden stream.*

*Here, amid the wild chorus,
we become both audience and author—
our hearts sketching verses
with every breath, every pause,
writing our own tale in the language of nature.*

Storytelling with Nature

As your journey through *Wild Stillness* continues, you've been deepening your connection to the natural world through presence, breath, heart, the senses, and creativity. With each chapter, you've softened more into yourself—opening, listening, expressing, and engaging with the land in gentle and meaningful ways. Now, this chapter invites something new to arise: your *story*.

We all carry stories—some remembered, some hidden, some waiting patiently to be spoken. These stories are not just about our past, but about how we see the world, how we feel, and what we're discovering along the way. When we walk through nature with presence, we begin to notice symbols, patterns, and encounters that feel strangely personal—as if the land is speaking to us in a language we almost remember.

This chapter is an invitation to *weave your own meaning* with the natural world. When you allow yourself to wonder, to imagine, to create stories, poems, and reflections inspired by nature, you begin to give voice to the emotional and symbolic layers of your experience. These aren't just playful activities (though they are that too); they're ways of understanding yourself more deeply. Nature becomes a co-author, helping you to unlock insights, emotions, and memories you may not have accessed otherwise. Finding your own rhythm, your own imagery, your own truth.

Storytelling with Nature in Ancient Wisdom

Storytelling is one of the oldest ways humans have made meaning of the world—and in ancient traditions across the globe, nature has always been at the heart of these stories. Long before books or screens, people looked to the land, the sky, the animals and elements for guidance, symbolism, and connection. The trees, the rivers, the stars—each held lessons, each carried messages. Nature *was* the story.

In Indigenous Australian cultures, storytelling is not just a form of entertainment—it is a sacred act of passing on wisdom, law, identity, and connection to Country. Through songlines, oral stories, and art, the land is understood as a living library—every rock, tree, and landscape feature holding ancestral knowledge and deep cultural meaning. These stories are not created apart from nature, but *with* it, reflecting the unbreakable relationship between people and place.

In Celtic and Druidic traditions, animals, forests, and weather patterns were rich with metaphor and myth. The flight of a bird, the call of an owl, or the appearance of a stag in the woods were never seen as random—they were signs, invitations to pay attention, to reflect, and to align with the deeper rhythms of life.

In Eastern spiritual traditions, storytelling through parables, poetry, and nature-based imagery has long been a tool for awakening. The moon, the lotus, the flowing river—all are symbols used to express spiritual truths. The natural world became the canvas for teaching timeless lessons of impermanence and unity.

These traditions remind us that stories are not just something we tell *about* nature—they are something we discover *with* nature. When we listen deeply, when we notice the small signs and synchronicities, when we allow ourselves to respond through words or art, we step into an ancient way of being—one that recognises the world around us as intelligent, alive, and always in conversation.

Holding Space for Emotion Through Story

As you move through the practices in this chapter, you may find that not all stories come gently. Sometimes, as we express ourselves through nature—through reflection, writing, or creative play—memories or emotions rise to the surface. Our stories are layered. Some are tender, some joyful, and some carry pain, grief, or unresolved moments.

If this happens for you, know that you are not doing it wrong. In fact, this is part of the process. Healing begins when we allow what's within us to come into the light—*not to relive it*, but to gently release it. Nature offers the perfect companion for this kind of release. It does not judge or hurry you. It simply receives, just as it has done for countless beings before you.

If a strong feeling arises, pause. Breathe. Place your hand on your heart or on the earth beneath you. Let yourself feel what is present—gently, slowly, without forcing. And when you're ready, you might imagine offering the feeling back to the land. A leaf can carry your grief. A stream can wash your sorrow. A breeze can take your words and let them fly free. Letting go is not about forgetting—it's about no longer carrying the weight alone.

Be kind to yourself through this process. Meet your inner world with the same softness you bring to a sunset or a wildflower. You are worthy of that tenderness. And know, always, that nature holds you in this. The earth has a vast, quiet strength that can hold your truth—every part of it. You don't need to be fixed. You don't need to have the right words. Just allowing what is here to be felt, honoured, and slowly released is enough.

This too, is storytelling. And this too, is healing.

As you explore the practices in this chapter, know that you are stepping into this lineage of meaning-making. Whether you shape a poem from leaves, tell a story through stones, or reflect on a moment with a tree—what matters is not the form, but the *feeling*.

Let nature be your muse, your mirror, and your co-author. There are stories waiting to be told. Some are already inside you. Others are whispered on the wind.

Leaf Collage Narrative

Nature holds stories in every leaf, branch, and stone, waiting to be noticed and expressed. In this practice, you gather leaves of different shapes, colours, and textures and use them as elements of a visual story.

- Encourages creative storytelling using natural elements as symbolic characters or events.
- Cultivates mindfulness by observing the details of leaves

A variety of leaves.
Paper or journal page
Glue, pens, markers

Intention: "I let the patterns and textures of nature inspire a story that flows from my heart to the land."

Head out on a slow, mindful walk and let yourself be drawn to the details underfoot and overhead. As you wander, begin gathering leaves that speak to you. Let your hands choose with curiosity. Once your pockets or basket are full, find a quiet space to sit and create. Spread your leaves out and take a moment to really notice them. Look at their shapes, their textures, the stories they already seem to hold. Do you see a face in that one? A wing? A forest path?

Now, begin arranging them on your paper —without overthinking. Let the leaves guide you into a story. Maybe they become a landscape, a character, or a moment from your own life. Trust the process and let your imagination lead. When your collage feels complete, you can gently secure the leaves in place with glue or tape. But more importantly, listen: What are the leaves saying? What story have they helped you tell?

Take a moment to write. It might be a short story, a poem, or just a few lines of reflection. Let the shapes and your arrangement inspire the words. What message lives inside this little forest of fragments?

This is storytelling with nature—quiet, creative, and deeply personal. And it reminds us that stories don't always begin with words. Sometimes, they begin with the falling of a leaf.

What story emerged from your leaf collage?
Was it one from your own journey, or did nature inspire something new?

Revisit the practice with a new theme—perhaps creating a leaf collage inspired by a myth or a dream.

Pebble Stories

Gather small pebbles and arrange them into an image. Use it as a spark for a short mindful story—whether by writing or illustrating—that reflects your inner thoughts and connection with nature. This exercise invites you to blend visual creativity with narrative reflection.

 *Outcomes*
- Enhances your sensory awareness and mindfulness by focusing on subtle details.
- Encourages creative expression through the integration of visual art and storytelling.

 *Items*
A collection of small pebbles gathered from nature
Paper and a pen or pencil

Intention: "I create a story woven from the earth's quiet wisdom."

 *Steps*

Take a slow, mindful walk with a curious heart. As you go, begin to notice the little things—especially the small pebbles that dot the path or nestle into the earth. Pick up a few that catch your eye. Find a peaceful spot to sit. Lay out your pebbles and begin to arrange them into a picture or a pattern. You might not know what you're making at first—that's okay. Let the shapes guide you.

Once your image takes form, pause. Take a few deep breaths and simply observe what you've made. What do you see? What emotions stir as you sit with this creation? Let the story start to form—not with pressure, but with presence.

Now, pick up your journal and let the words or drawings come. Write a short story, a reflection, or a poem inspired by your pebble arrangement. It might tell the tale of a quiet moment, a memory, or a character that emerged unexpectedly from the shapes you created. Or it might just be a feeling made visible. Let the process be playful and honest. You don't need to plan—just follow what flows. When you're finished, take a moment to read over or look at what you've created. It's more than just stones on the ground—it's a reflection of your inner world, spoken through the language of the land. Let it remind you that even the smallest things can hold big stories.

 *Reflect*
What did you notice about the image you created?
What emotions or memories surfaced during this process?

 *More*
Experiment with rearranging the pebbles at different time to explore how changing formations inspire new narrative

Rock Portraits

Every rock holds a story—a journey shaped by time, weather, and the landscape it has traveled through. In this practice, you choose a smooth stone and transform it into a character or symbol of meaning. Through painting or decorating, you bring its story to life.

- Encourages creative storytelling through a tangible, nature-based object.
- Cultivates mindfulness by inviting deeper interaction with natural elements.

A smooth stone.
Paint, markers, paper

Intention: "I bring awareness to the faces and forms hidden in stone."

As you walk slowly through nature, let your eyes search the ground for a stone that seems to call to you. Take your time choosing one that feels right—like it holds a story waiting to be told. Sit down somewhere quiet and hold the stone gently in your hands. Feel its texture, shape, and temperature. Where might it have come from? Has it rested in a riverbed, been shaped by wind, or tumbled down a hillside over years? Let your imagination wander through its past.

Now, using paint or markers, begin to decorate the stone. You might add symbols that reflect who you are—spirals, stars, waves—or patterns that represent memories, dreams, or feelings. You might even draw small images that feel like pieces of your inner world. Let the act of decorating become a meditation in itself—slow, intentional, and expressive.

When your rock portrait is complete, place it in front of you and begin to write. Let the rock speak. Where has it travelled? What ancient lands has it known? What message might it carry for you now? Write freely and curiously, blending your own story with the imagined journey of the stone. This practice is more than art—it's a conversation with the land and with yourself. A reminder that every stone holds time, and sometimes, our hearts just need a quiet moment to listen.

*What drew you to this particular stone?
How did the act of painting and writing deepen your connection with the stone's story?*

Consider creating a "rock journal" where you collect and document the imagined lives of different stones.

Soundscape Storytelling

Nature speaks in whispers, rhythms, and echoes—a living symphony of sound that carries its own untold stories. In this practice, you will record the natural soundscape of a place that calls to you. Then invite these sounds to become the foundation of a story.

 **Outcomes**
- Develops deep listening skills and awareness of nature's subtle, ever-changing voices.
- Encourages creative storytelling by transforming sounds into narrative elements.

 **Items**
A phone or recording device
Paper and pen

Intention: "I listen deeply to the sounds around me, letting nature's voice guide the story."

 **Steps**

Find a natural spot where you can sit quietly for a little while. Settle in and close your eyes, letting the world around you come alive through sound. Take a few deep breaths and begin to listen—not just with your ears, but with your whole attention. Notice the near and the far: a bird calling close by, leaves rustling overhead, perhaps the distant hum of insects or the rhythm of water. Let the layers build like music.

When you feel ready, press record. Let your device capture the moment—not just the sounds, but the mood, the rhythm, the aliveness of the space. You don't need to speak—just let nature tell its own story for a few minutes.

Once you've recorded, play it back. Close your eyes if you'd like, and listen again—but this time, imagine. Who's making these sounds? What kind of world are you hearing? Could the wind be whispering secrets? Is that bird delivering a message? Is the creek giggling, or warning, or guiding?

Now, open your journal and begin to write. Let a story unfold—maybe a tale of forest creatures, or a hidden village deep in the trees. Maybe it's a poem from the perspective of the wind. Let nature's voice become your creative muse.

 **Reflect**
What emotions or images did the sounds evoke as you listened? How did translating the soundscape into a story shift your awareness of nature?

 **More**
Try this practice in different environments and compare the stories that emerge from each setting.

Letter to Nature

Nature is a patient listener, holding the stories of the world in its roots, rivers, and stones. In this practice, write a personal letter to a part of nature that calls to you—a tree that has offered shade, or a river that has carried your thoughts.

- Deepens your personal connection with nature by treating it as a living, listening presence.
- Encourages emotional reflection and storytelling through letter writing.

A journal or paper.
A pen or pencil.
A quiet outdoor space.

Intention: "I write to the land, offering my words as an expression of connection and respect."

Find a quiet place where you can sit with a part of nature that holds meaning for you. Settle into stillness and take a few deep breaths. Close your eyes for a moment and feel into your connection with this natural being. Let the memories rise—moments of comfort, joy, awe, or even grief that you've shared.

Now, open your notebook and begin to write a letter. Just as you would to a close friend, let your words flow honestly and warmly. You might start with "Dear River," or "Hello Old Tree." Tell your chosen part of nature how it's made you feel, what it has shown you, or how its presence has shaped your journey. Maybe you share a memory, ask a question, or simply offer thanks. Let the words be personal and open—as if the land could truly hear and hold your story.

When your letter feels complete, take a quiet moment to read it—aloud if you feel comfortable, or silently, from your heart. Let yourself feel the connection, like a thread woven between you and the living world.

You can choose to keep your letter tucked in a journal or return it to the earth—placing it beneath a stone, burying it gently, or leaving it where the wind can carry it. This is your way of saying: I see you. I remember. I belong here, too.

How did writing a letter to nature change the way you see it? What emotions surfaced as you expressed your thoughts?

Respond to your letter from nature's perspective, allowing yourself to imagine the wisdom it would share with you .

Wildflower Poem

Wildflowers bloom freely, untamed and unbound, each one carrying its own quiet story. In this practice, you immerse yourself in the presence of wildflowers—observing their colours, movement, and the way they harmonise with the land. Then put your experience into words.

 **Outcomes**
- Encourages creative self-expression through poetry inspired by nature.
- Cultivates mindfulness by deepening your observation of wildflowers and their beauty.

 **Items**
A natural setting with wildflowers
Pen and paper

Intention: "I let the beauty of wildflowers inspire my words."

 **Steps**

Wander until you find a place where wildflowers bloom freely. Choose a spot where you can sit quietly among them, undisturbed. Take a few deep, gentle breaths and allow your senses to soften. Look closely at the flowers around you—their colours, shapes, and how they move with the breeze. Notice the way they lean toward the light, how some stand tall while others curl delicately toward the earth.

Now, tune in to how these wildflowers make you feel. Do they spark a memory? Stir a feeling? Whisper something you can't quite put into words yet? Let yourself sit in that quiet space where observation meets emotion.

When you're ready, open your journal and begin writing. Let the poem unfold naturally, like petals opening in the sun. Don't worry about form or rhyme—just let the words bloom as they wish. Write about what you see, but more importantly, write about what you feel: the freedom, the stillness, the resilience, or the wild joy held in a single flower's curve.

When you've finished, take a moment to read your poem aloud—just to yourself. Let your own voice carry the imagery and feeling you captured. This is your way of honouring the flowers, and the part of you that felt something deep and true in their presence.

 **Reflect**

How did the presence of wildflowers influence your emotions or thoughts?
What themes emerged in your poem—freedom, growth, resilience, beauty?

 **More**

Consider pressing a wildflower into your journal alongside your poem as a keepsake.

Animal Encounter

Every encounter with an animal in the wild is a moment of connection—an unspoken exchange between two beings sharing the earth. In this practice, you reflect on a time when you crossed paths with an animal, whether a fleeting glance or a profound interaction.

- Deepens your sense of connection with the natural world through personal storytelling.
- Encourages reflection on the wisdom animals offer through their presence and behaviour.

A journal or paper.
A pen or pencil.
A quiet space for reflection.

Intention: "I reflect on the wisdom that animals share, allowing their presence to teach me."

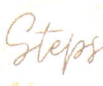

Think back to a time when you had a quiet moment with an animal in the wild. Maybe it was a bird that landed close and lingered longer than expected, a curious insect that crawled across your hand, or a kangaroo or deer pausing to meet your gaze from a distance. It doesn't need to be dramatic—just a moment that made you pause and notice. Find a peaceful spot and close your eyes. Let yourself return to that memory. Where were you? What time of day was it? What sounds or smells surrounded you? Picture the animal—what was it doing? How did it move? What kind of energy did it carry?

Now, open your notebook and begin writing. Describe the encounter in as much detail as you can. Let the story unfold slowly—draw your reader into the moment. Then, begin to reflect. What did that experience stir in you? Did you feel seen, comforted, surprised? Was there a sense of connection—like the animal knew you were there and didn't mind?

Allow your writing to explore any meaning the moment holds. Perhaps it shifted your perspective, reminded you of something forgotten, or simply grounded you in the wonder of being alive. Let it be honest. Let it be yours.

When you've finished, read your story back to yourself. Notice how it feels to hold that memory again, to honour it through words. Sometimes the animals we meet aren't just part of the scenery—they're silent messengers, reminding us of the wildness and gentleness still alive within us.

How did this animal encounter make you feel in the moment?
What qualities did the animal embody that you admire or relate to?

Try writing from the perspective of the animal—how might it have perceived the encounter?

Free-Flow Writing

Nature holds space for unfiltered expression, offering an open landscape where thoughts can roam freely. In this practice, you let your words flow without restriction as you sit immersed in nature. Describe what you see, reflect on emotions, or let your mind wander.

 *Outcomes*
- Encourages creative expression and self-discovery through free-writing.
- Cultivates mindfulness by bringing full presence to nature and your thoughts.

 *Items*
A journal or notebook.
A pen or pencil.
A quiet outdoor space.

Intention: "I release expectations and let my words move like the wind, flowing naturally and freely."

 *Steps*

Find a quiet spot in nature where you feel calm and uninterrupted. Let the stillness of the space surround you as you settle in. Take a few deep, steady breaths. Feel your body soften and your senses begin to tune into the world around you—the light, the air, the scents and sounds. Let yourself arrive fully, without rush.

When you're ready open your notebook and begin to write. Let your pen move freely across the page, describing whatever comes to mind. You might write about what you see around you, what's stirring inside you, or slip into a memory or story that begins to unfold on its own.

There's no need to filter or correct. This isn't about crafting perfect sentences—it's about letting your inner voice meet the outer world. Even if all you write is "I don't know what to write," keep the pen moving. Often, what needs to be said comes through once we begin.

When it feels complete, pause. Take a breath. Then read back over your words, slowly and without judgment. What do you notice? Are there repeating ideas, a mood, a thread of thought that surprises you? Let this practice be a window into your own unfolding—shaped by nature, shaped by stillness, shaped by the quiet invitation to simply write what's true in the moment.

 *Reflect*
What surprised you about what emerged in your writing?
How did sitting in nature influence your thoughts and creativity?

 *More*
Turn your free-writing into a poem or short story.

Night Sky Narrative

The night sky has long been a source of wonder, storytelling, and deep reflection. In this practice, you sit beneath the stars and allow their quiet presence to guide your writing. Whether you imagine a celestial journey, reflect on your place in the universe, or write about the whispers of the night, this exercise invites you to blend creativity with awe.

- Encourages creative storytelling and reflection through connection with the cosmos.
- Cultivates mindfulness by immersing you in the stillness of the night sky.

A journal, pen or pencil.
A quiet outdoor space with a clear view of the night sky.

Intention: "I allow my imagination to wander, finding stories in the constellations above."

Find a quiet outdoor space where you can lie back or sit comfortably beneath the night sky. Let yourself settle into the darkness, breathing slowly as the sky stretches out above you. Take a few deep, grounding breaths and allow the stillness of night to wrap around you. Gaze gently at the stars. Notice their quiet flicker, the patterns they form, and the endless space that holds them. Let yourself feel small—in the most beautiful way.

When your mind begins to wander, follow it. Open your notebook and begin to write. There's no set direction—just let the stars guide you. Maybe a story begins to form, sparked by a constellation or a shimmer in the sky. Maybe you reflect on the mystery of the universe and your place in it. Or maybe you write simply about how this moment feels—quiet, open, infinite.

Let the words come as they do. No editing, no judgment. Just your thoughts, flowing like starlight onto the page. When you feel finished, pause. Reread what you've written. Let it sink in. Notice what surprised you, what truths slipped in while your eyes were on the sky.

This is your story, shaped by the cosmos—a reminder that even in the vast silence above, your voice has a place, and your presence matters.

Reflect
How did sitting under the night sky influence your thoughts and emotions?
Did your writing explore themes of wonder, connection, or mystery?

Try this practice on different nights, observing how the changing sky influences your writing.

Personal Totem

Throughout history, humans have formed deep connections with objects found in nature, seeing them as symbols of guidance, protection, or transformation. In this practice, you seek out a natural object that resonates with you —and honour it as a personal totem.

 *Outcomes*
- Deepens your personal connection with nature through symbolism and storytelling.
- Encourages mindfulness by bringing awareness to the meanings and emotions tied to natural objects.

 *Items*
A natural object that speaks to you.
A journal or paper.
A pen or pencil

Intention: "I connect with the energy of a chosen object, letting it hold a personal meaning for me."

 *Steps*

Take a slow, mindful walk through nature. Don't look for anything in particular—just stay open to what calls to you. Sooner or later, something will catch your attention. It might be a curved stick, a worn feather, a stone with a surprising shape. When you find it, pause. Pick it up. Feel it in your hands.

Notice its texture, weight, and the way it rests in your palm. Why this object? What drew you to it? Sometimes it's a quiet pull—something unspoken that just feels right.

Find a peaceful spot to sit with your chosen totem. Let your thoughts settle and begin to reflect: What does this object represent to you? Does it hold the energy of strength, transformation, patience, or something else entirely? Is there a memory it stirs, or a message it seems to offer?

Now open your journal and begin to write. Describe your totem and what it means to you. Let the story flow—why you picked it, how it mirrors a part of your journey, and what lessons it might carry for the path ahead.

When you're finished, you might want to place your totem somewhere special—in your home, on an altar, in a pocket or pouch. Let it be a quiet reminder of your connection to the land and to your own unfolding story. A symbol of the wisdom that nature shares, when we're willing to listen.

 *Reflect*
What drew you to this particular object?
How does it reflect something within you or your current journey?

 *More*
Craft a small altar or display with your totems as a way to honour your connection with nature's wisdom.

Time Capsule Story

Just as nature evolves through the seasons, so do we. This practice invites you to create a time capsule—choosing a natural object that represents your present state and pairing it with a written reflection. By burying or storing it in a special place, you create a marker in time.

- Encourages self-reflection by capturing a moment in time .
- Fosters mindfulness and patience by allowing time to pass before revisiting the capsule.

A natural object.
Paper and a pen or pencil.
A place to bury or store your time capsule safely

Intention: "I honour this moment by capturing it in words."

Find a quiet moment to pause and gently check in with yourself. Where are you in your life right now? What emotions are sitting close? Are there challenges you're facing or hopes you're quietly holding onto? Once you've had a moment to reflect, take a slow walk in nature and let yourself be drawn to an object that symbolises this moment in time for you. It might be a fallen leaf, a smooth stone, a feather, or a shell—something simple, but meaningful.

Now, sit somewhere still and begin writing a note to your future self. Describe how you're feeling, what you're learning, and any questions or dreams that feel alive in you right now. Let the words be honest—this letter is just for you. When you're finished, fold the note and place it alongside your chosen object. You can bury them gently in a safe place (being mindful of the environment), or tuck them away in a special box, drawer, or jar at home.

Choose a date—maybe a season from now, or even a year ahead—to return to your time capsule. When the moment comes, open it slowly and read your words. Hold the object again and feel into what's changed... and what hasn't.

This practice is a gentle gift to yourself—a way to honour where you've been, where you are, and where you're still becoming. A reminder that growth happens quietly, just like in nature. One season at a time.

How did the natural object you chose reflect your state of being at the time?
What emotions arose when revisiting your time capsule?

Repeat this practice at different life stages or seasonal shifts, collecting multiple time capsules over time .

Nature Dialogue

Nature holds wisdom in its stillness, movement, and quiet presence. In this practice, you choose a natural element and engage in a spoken dialogue with it. Imagine it as a wise guide, listening deeply and offering quiet responses in the language of nature.

- Encourages deep listening and presence with the natural world.
- Develops self-awareness by expressing thoughts

A quiet outdoor space
A journal or paper.

Intention: "I listen with an open heart, allowing the land, the wind, and the trees to speak."

Find a quiet, undisturbed place where you can sit with a natural presence that draws you in. Settle in and take a few slow, grounding breaths. Let yourself tune into the presence of your chosen element. Notice its stillness, its movement, its energy. Feel as though you're sitting with an old, wise friend. When you feel ready, begin to speak aloud. Share what's on your mind—your thoughts, your questions, your hopes or heaviness. Speak as if the tree, river, rock, or breeze is truly listening. There's no need to censor or rehearse—just let the words come honestly and gently.

After each thought, pause. Breathe. Listen—not necessarily for words, but for a feeling, an image, a sensation, or even a subtle change in the air. Sometimes nature replies in silence; sometimes in a rustling leaf or a shift in light.

Let the conversation unfold at its own pace. You might feel comforted, surprised, or simply still. Imagine what this natural element would say if it could speak. What wisdom might it carry from its many years of simply being?

When you feel complete, offer a quiet thank you to your nature mentor. Before you leave, take a moment to jot down what arose—insights, feelings, or images that stayed with you. This is your reminder that we are never alone in nature. The land listens, and sometimes, it gently answers back.

What natural element did you choose, and why did it call to you?
How did speaking aloud change the way you processed your thoughts?

Try this practice with different elements—speak to the wind one day, a river another, and a mountain the next.

A Moment of Reflection

Before moving forward, take a moment to reflect on your journey weaving stories with the land.

How did it feel to express yourself through storytelling with nature? Did it bring a sense of playfulness, reflection, or deeper connection?
___
___
___

What did nature reveal to you through these practices? Did any particular landscape, element, or object spark a story, memory, or insight?
___
___
___

Did you discover something unexpected about yourself or your relationship with nature? How did it feel to let your creativity and emotions take shape through storytelling?
___
___
___

What was it like to tell your own story through nature's lens? Did you feel a sense of belonging, healing, or deeper self-awareness?
___
___
___

Do you feel ready to move forward? The next chapter invites you into the practice of impermanence—creating and releasing, giving without holding on. Does this feel like a natural next step?

Take your time. Let the stories continue to unfold within you, knowing that nature holds an endless well of inspiration.

Chapter 7:
Leaving No Trace

*In a world where every step fades,
our art becomes a whisper on the wind—
a gentle dance of form and fleeting grace.*

*Here, nature is our canvas,
its ever-changing hues and textures
reminding us that nothing lasts,
and in that impermanence, there is freedom.*

*Our creations are moments,
like dewdrops that vanish at dawn—
brief reflections of our love for the earth,
crafted with care, then offered back
to the wild, unburdened and pure.*

*In leaving no trace, we honour
the cycle of birth, decay, and renewal—
a gentle reminder that true art
lives in the heart, not on the surface.*

The Beauty of Impermanence

So far, your Wild Stillness journey has led you through deepening layers of connection—with presence, with breath, with heart, with senses, and through creative expression. You've listened, played, expressed, and reflected. Now, this chapter invites a subtle but powerful shift: to create and connect *without holding on*.

This is the art of impermanence—of engaging with nature fully, but gently, leaving no trace of your presence except for the energy and attention you brought to it. In a world that often celebrates permanence, achievement, and possession, this is a quiet rebellion. To make something beautiful, knowing it will fade. To leave behind no mark except gratitude.

Creating in this way is not less meaningful—it's often *more*. Because when we know that a sculpture made of sticks will be blown away, or a mandala made of petals will be scattered by the wind, we're invited into the *pure experience* of the moment. We let go of control. We let go of outcome. We return to presence, and trust that the act itself—the attention, the care, the joy—is enough.

Leaving No Trace in Ancient Wisdom

Long before "Leave No Trace" became a modern environmental ethic, it was already woven into the way ancient peoples lived with the earth. In traditional cultures across the world—including Indigenous Australian wisdom—there was no concept of ownership over nature, only *relationship*. The land was not something to be used, but something to be *respected*, *listened to*, and *cared for*.

Every action was taken with deep awareness: where to walk, what to harvest, how to move through a place without disturbing it. Tracks were tread lightly, fires were tended with reverence, and sacred places were visited only with permission—offered not by people, but by the land itself. To walk gently was not just practical—it was spiritual. It was an acknowledgment that the earth is alive, and that we are not above it, but part of it.

In First Nations Australian culture, this deep respect is expressed in the understanding of *Country* as a living being—one that holds ancestral knowledge, spirit, and identity. To mark it carelessly or take from it without giving back is to break that relationship. In traditional practices, people would sit quietly, observe the signs of the land, and always leave a place as it was.

In Buddhist and Hindu traditions, the principle of *ahimsa*—non-harming—extends beyond people to include animals, plants, and even the subtle energies of place. Monks would sweep the path before walking so as not to step on small insects. Ritual offerings were made from natural elements that would return to the earth. There was an understanding that the world is not inert—it is sacred.

These ancient ways remind us that "leaving no trace" isn't about disappearing—it's about belonging. It's about being so present, so respectful, and so attuned to the land that your presence becomes part of its balance, not a disruption to it.

Gathering Sustainably: Creating with Care

When working with natural materials in ephemeral and eco-art, it is essential to gather sustainably—taking only what is already loose, abundant, or naturally fallen, and ensuring that our creative process does not disturb the balance of the environment. Sustainable gathering means being mindful of the ecosystems we interact with, respecting living plants and creatures, and choosing materials that can return to the earth without harm. Before collecting stones, shells, leaves, or other elements, ask yourself: Is this plentiful in this area? Will removing it impact the landscape or wildlife? By approaching nature with care and gratitude, we honour its generosity while leaving no trace—allowing the land to continue thriving long after our art has faded.

Letting Go with Nature's Wisdom

As you create with the land—knowing your artwork will be reshaped, scattered, or dissolved—you are also practicing something much deeper: the art of *letting go*. In life, we often try to hold on tightly. To control outcomes, to fix what feels uncertain, to resist change. But just like the petals in your mandala, or the sticks in your sculpture, some things are not meant to stay.

Nature shows us this truth every day. The leaves fall. The tide returns. The storm passes. Everything moves in cycles—rising, falling, beginning again. When we create something beautiful and then watch the wind carry it away, we begin to feel this rhythm in our own lives. We remember that we, too, are part of these cycles. And that not everything needs to be held so tightly.

When worries arise, or life doesn't unfold as we hoped, we can gently shift our perspective. We can step back, take a breath, and see the situation not as a failure or burden, but as part of a bigger unfolding—one we don't always have to understand. Just like the artwork you leave behind in the forest, some moments are meant to be released.

In doing so, we create space—for healing, for trust, for something new. We learn to flow with life, not against it. To soften instead of grip. And we discover a quiet kind of freedom—not from having everything under control, but from knowing we don't need to. So when your next worry comes, imagine it as a leaf placed gently in a stream. Watch it float. Let it go. Nature will carry it, just as it carries you.

Let the rain take it.
Let the earth receive it.
Let it return to where it came from.

Gratitude Mandalas

A mandala is a circle of harmony, a reflection of wholeness, a moment woven into nature. In this practice, you gather leaves, petals, stones—each one a quiet offering of gratitude. With each piece your mandala becomes a prayer of appreciation.

 *Outcomes*
- Cultivates gratitude and mindfulness through creative expression.
- Encourages awareness of natural patterns and materials

 *Items*
Leaves, stones, flowers, twigs, shells, or other natural objects
A flat outdoor surface.

Intention: "I create with gratitude, knowing that beauty exists in the moment, not in permanence."

 *Steps*

Find a quiet outdoor space where you can be undisturbed. Take a few deep breaths and gently reflect on the things, people, and moments in your life that you're grateful for. Begin gathering natural materials from the area around you. Look for leaves, pebbles, twigs, flower petals, or anything that has already fallen. Choose with care, noticing the shapes, textures, and colours that draw you in. This is part of the practice—moving slowly, with appreciation.

When you're ready, begin placing your materials in a circle, starting from the centre and working outward. Let the pattern unfold naturally—there's no right or wrong way. With each piece you place, silently offer a thank you. It might be for a friend, a recent experience, your breath, or even the beauty of the leaf in your hand.

Let this quiet act of creation be a meditation—a way to honour what you love, while being fully present with the land. When your mandala feels complete, take a step back. Observe the details, the balance, the small perfections. Let it be a reflection of your inner state and the beauty of impermanence.

Then leave it right where it is—as a gift to the earth. Let the wind, rain, or time carry it away, just as all things in nature eventually return. What remains is the gratitude you've offered, **and the stillness you've created in the process.**

 *Reflect*
How did it feel to express gratitude through art?
What patterns or shapes naturally formed in your mandala?

 *More*
Return to the same location in different seasons to create new mandalas using what's naturally available.

Breathing Brushstrokes

Like clouds drifting across the sky, your breath is a movement, a quiet act of creation. In this practice you paint with water letting each brushstroke rise and fade with the flow of your breath. As the strokes slowly disappear you are reminded of the art of letting go.

 **Outcomes**
- Develops focus and body awareness through mindful breathing.
- Encourages creative self-expression using natural elements.

 **Items**
A small container of water
A feather or a smooth stick
A flat surface

Intention: "I let each breath guide my movement, painting with air, water, and presence."

 **Steps**

Find a quiet outdoor space with a smooth surface to paint on. Bring a small container of water and a brush, feather, or even a twig that feels nice in your hand. Before you begin, take a moment to stand or sit still. Inhale slowly, then gently exhale, noticing how your body softens. Let your breath guide you into presence.

Dip your feather or stick into the water, and as you exhale, make a brushstroke on the surface. Let the motion match your breath—slow, flowing, unhurried. Inhale again, and with the next exhale, make another mark.

Keep going, exploring different movements, shapes, and patterns. Try looping, sweeping, dotting, or flowing lines. You might switch hands or change your position. Let your body respond to what feels natural.

As the water begins to evaporate, watch your brushstrokes slowly disappear. There's something peaceful in that—in making art that doesn't stay, that lives in the moment and fades with the wind and sun.

Let this practice remind you that not all beauty needs to be held onto. Sometimes, it's enough to create, breathe, and simply let go.

 **Reflect**
How did it feel to match your brushstrokes to your breath? What did you notice about your focus and emotions during the activity?

 **More**
Try this activity using different tools, like leaves or flowers to explore new textures.

Stone Stacking

Like mountains shaped by time, each stone holds a story—of weight, balance, and belonging. In this practice, you carefully stack and arrange stones, feeling their texture, their edges, their quiet presence in your hands.

 **Outcomes**
- Enhances your mindfulness and sensory awareness.
- Encourages creative self-expression and reflection through the decoration of your stone stack.

 **Items** — A selection of stones

Intention: "I balance each stone, honouring the delicate harmony between stillness and impermanence."

 **Steps**

Head out to a natural space where you can safely gather a few stones. Choose mindfully, collecting stones that vary in size, shape, and texture. Let your hands do the choosing, guided by curiosity and care for the land.

Find a flat surface nearby and begin to arrange your stones. Stack them slowly and gently, one on top of the other. Notice how they rest in relationship to one another, adjusting and experimenting until you find balance. Let this be a quiet meditation. As you work, feel your breath steadying, your awareness deepening. You might create tall towers, spirals, or low, balanced circles—whatever form emerges is perfect.

Once your arrangement feels complete, take a step back and simply observe. Notice the way each stone contributes to the whole, and how easily the entire structure could shift or fall. Reflect on how this mirrors your own moments of balance, and the ever-changing nature of things.

When you're ready, decide whether to gently dismantle your creation, returning the stones to where you found them—or leave it knowing the wind, rain, or time will eventually carry it away. This is your quiet offering to the earth—an art of balance, presence, and letting go.

 **Reflect**

How did the process of stacking and decorating the stones affect your sense of focus and calm?
What challenges did you encounter while seeking balance, and what did they teach you about patience?

 **More**

Invite a friend or family member to join you in a collaborative stone stacking session.

Zen Sand Designs

With each stroke in the sand, you create—a pattern, a moment, a reflection of presence. The grains shift beneath your touch, forming lines and curves that exist only for now. This practice is a quiet dance with impermanence, a reminder that nothing is fixed.

- Enhances mindfulness by engaging you in slow, intentional movement.
- Encourages emotional release and acceptance of impermanence

Outdoor space with a flat, soft patch of sand
A stick or similar natural tool

Intention: "I trace patterns in the sand, embracing the beauty of letting go."

Find a peaceful outdoor spot where there's a patch of soft sand. Settle in comfortably and take a few deep, grounding breaths. Feel the air, the light, and the quiet around you.

Pick up a stick, feather, or your finger, and begin to draw slowly in the sand. Let your movements be deliberate and unhurried. Maybe you create spirals, lines, waves, or a mandala. There's no right or wrong—just follow what feels good in the moment.

Listen to the gentle scratch as the tool moves through the sand. Feel the texture under your hand. Let your awareness rest fully on this act of creating—just you, the sand, and the moment.

When you feel ready, gently smooth over your design with your palm or a soft brush. Let it be a soft letting go. Imagine any thoughts or feelings you no longer need dissolving with the lines—like waves smoothing the shore.

Begin again with a fresh design if you wish. This practice is all about cycles—creating, releasing, beginning anew. A quiet reminder that nothing in nature is held forever, and there is beauty in each fleeting shape we leave behind.

How did the slow, deliberate movement affect your state of mind and body?
What sensations did you notice as you created your pattern and then smoothed it away?

Try this practice in different natural settings—such as on a beach or a garden path.

Nature Collage

Wander slowly through the landscape, letting your senses guide you. A smooth stone, a curled leaf, a feather in the grass—each small treasure catches your eye for a reason. Gather what speaks to you and arrange them into a collage, a fleeting expression of the moment.

Outcomes
- Enhances your sensory awareness by encouraging you to notice beauties of nature.
- Fosters mindfulness and creative self-expression through the reflective process of collage.

Items
A natural outdoor setting for gathering small objects
A small bag or container

Intention: "I gather fallen leaves, petals, and twigs, weaving them into a story that belongs to the land."

Steps

Take your time as you wander through a natural space. Let your senses guide you, and collect small items that draw your attention. Maybe it's a curled bark, a delicate feather, a fallen blossom, or a speckled stone. Choose gently and only what has already fallen, being mindful not to disturb the environment. When your hands feel full or your heart says it's time, find a quiet place to pause. A flat rock, a tree stump, or a patch of earth will do just fine. Lay out your treasures in front of you and begin to arrange them.

Let the process be slow and intuitive. Move pieces around. Notice how their colours, shapes, and textures work together. Let the collage form itself—not with a plan, but with presence. As you place each item, pause and reflect—why did this piece catch your eye? What does it remind you of? A feeling? A season? A memory?

When your arrangement feels complete, simply sit with it. Take in the beauty, the balance, and what it reveals about what you were drawn to in this moment. And when you're ready to move on, consider leaving the collage where it is as a quiet gift to the land—or gently scatter the pieces back into their place, letting nature continue its own slow dance of change.

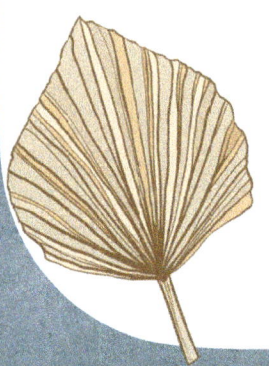

Reflect
How did collecting and arranging these natural objects influence your awareness of the environment?
What specific qualities in each object caught your attention and why?

More
Try creating a new collage in a different season to observe how your focus on nature's details evolves over time .

Driftwood Mandalas

Walk along the shoreline collecting weathered driftwood. Each piece carries a story of water and wind, shaped by time and tide. Gather those that call to you and arrange them in a circular pattern, balancing their forms into a mandala of harmony.

 *Outcomes*
- Develops spatial awareness and an understanding of symmetry in design.
- Encourages mindfulness through slow, intentional placement of objects.

 *Items*
Small pieces of driftwood
A flat surface (sand, soil, or a large rock)

Intention: "I arrange driftwood in a sacred circle, trusting that waves will return them to their journey."

 *Steps*

Take a slow, quiet walk along a beach, lakeshore, or riverbank. Let yourself move without urgency, keeping an eye out for small pieces of driftwood—those sun-bleached, water-smoothed fragments shaped by time and tide. As you collect, notice the textures, the bends, the feel of each one in your hand. When you've gathered enough, find a flat, open space where you can sit and create without interruption. Begin by placing one piece in the centre. Then slowly build outward, arranging the driftwood in a circular pattern. Let your hands move with care and attention.

Choose each piece mindfully. Feel its weight. Notice its grain and curve. Aim for balance—not perfection. Arrange the pieces in a way that feels steady and harmonious, adjusting spacing and direction as you go. Once your mandala feels complete, take a step back. Breathe. Let your eyes wander over the pattern, noticing how each individual piece contributes to the whole.

You might choose to leave your creation just as it is—an offering to the shore and the shifting tides. Or you can gently scatter the pieces back where they came from, allowing the wind and water to carry them on their next journey. Either way, you've created something beautiful and temporary—just like every moment we meet in nature.

 *Reflect*
How did it feel to arrange the driftwood into a balanced design?
Did you notice different textures, shapes, or colours as you worked?

 *More*
Explore how different materials influence the patterns and symmetry of your designs.

Mud Finger Painting

Experience the grounding and sensory connection of creating art with nature's own paint. Engage with the earth through mindful finger painting using natural mud. By feeling the texture, temperature, and movement of the mud, you cultivate a deeper sensory awareness.

 **Outcomes**
- Enhances sensory awareness through touch and texture.
- Encourages creativity using natural materials.

 **Items**
A small patch of natural mud (or soft, damp soil)
A flat rock, tree bark, natural canvas

Intention: "I connect with the earth through touch, allowing nature to be both my paint and my canvas."

 **Steps**

Find a spot outdoors where the soil is soft and welcoming. Add a little water and mix it gently with your fingers until it becomes a smooth, paint-like consistency. This is your natural palette—simple, grounding, and alive. Take a moment to explore the mud with your hands. Feel its texture, its coolness, the way it clings and shifts. There's no rush—this is as much about the sensation as it is about the creating.

Now, look around for a surface that feels right—a large rock, a fallen piece of bark, or even a bare patch of earth. Let your fingers become your brushes. Begin to paint, moving slowly and intuitively. You might create shapes, spirals, or a flowing abstract design. Let your hands follow whatever feels natural.

As the mud begins to dry, notice the changes—the cracks, the darkening or lightening of colour. This artwork isn't meant to last. And that's the beauty of it. It's about the moment, the touch, the quiet joy of creating something with the earth itself.

When you're done, rinse your hands in a nearby stream or rub them clean on grass or leaves. Let this be part of the ritual—a final act of connection and release. This is a practice of presence, play, and impermanence—reminding you that sometimes, the most meaningful art is the kind that leaves no trace at all.

 **Reflect**
How did it feel to create art using natural materials?
What did you notice about the texture of the mud on your hands?

 **More**
Incorporate small natural objects like leaves, twigs, or pebbles into your design.

Sand Mandala

A mandala is a sacred, circular design that symbolises wholeness, harmony, and the impermanence of life. In this practice, you create a mandala in the sand using natural materials such as stones, shells, or driftwood, knowing that the tide will soon carry it away.

 *Outcomes*
- Encourages mindfulness and presence by creating beauty that is meant to be temporary.
- Fosters a connection with nature's cycles of creation and release.

 *Items*
A quiet sandy area. Small natural objects such as shells, pebbles, or seaweed).

Intention: "I create a design in the sand, understanding that impermanence is part of the beauty."

 *Steps*

Find a peaceful stretch of sand. Pause for a moment before you begin. Take a deep breath and gently set an intention for your mandala. Perhaps it's peace, gratitude, or simply a quiet reflection. Using your hands or a stick, trace a large circle in the sand. This will be the foundation of your mandala—a sacred space for your creativity and presence to unfold.

Begin placing natural materials within the circle—small stones, shells, bits of driftwood or seaweed. Work from the centre outward, arranging your pieces in patterns that feel balanced and meaningful. Let symmetry guide you, but don't worry about perfection. This is a living artwork—just like you.

As you work, slow down. Feel the textures beneath your fingers, the warmth or coolness of the sand, the sound of nearby waves or breeze. Let this be a meditative practice—one that anchors you fully in the moment. When your mandala feels complete, take a few steps back and simply look. Notice the beauty you've created with such gentle presence.

And then, let it go. Leave your mandala right where it is and allow nature—wind, water, time—to carry it away. This is the quiet grace of ephemeral art: here for a moment, and then gone. Just like a breath.

 *Reflect*
How did it feel to create something knowing it would not last? What did this practice teach you about impermanence and letting go?

 *More*
Before leaving, set an intention that the waves carry your peace far and wide across the ocean.

Twig Sculptures

Nature is a constant cycle of growth, transformation, and return. In this practice, you gather fallen twigs and arrange them into small, free-form sculptures. Your creation might be abstract, resemble a figure, or take the shape of an animal or symbol.

 *Outcomes*
- Encourages creative expression while working in harmony with nature.
- Reinforces the practice of leaving no trace by using only natural, found materials.

 *Items*
Fallen twigs of various sizes

Intention: "I shape and weave twigs into form, knowing that nature will reclaim them in its own time."

 *Steps*

Take a slow, mindful wander through a natural area. As you walk, keep your eyes open for twigs that have already fallen to the ground. There's no need to snap or break anything living—nature always offers what you need if you're patient. When you feel ready, find a quiet spot where you can sit and work in peace. Lay out your twigs and take a moment to observe them. Notice their shapes, textures, curves, and lengths. Which ones fit naturally together? Which ones might balance or weave with others?

Begin arranging your sculpture. You might stack them carefully, balance them into towers or arches, or even interlock them to create a shape or pattern. There's no right or wrong—just follow your hands and curiosity. Let the form emerge slowly and intuitively.

Your sculpture might look like a little creature, a shelter, a spiral, or something entirely abstract. Whatever it becomes, let it carry your quiet attention and creative spirit. When it feels complete, pause and take it in. Appreciate the shape, the process, and your presence in making it. Then decide—do you want to leave it for others to find, just for a little while? Or would you prefer to gently scatter the twigs back into the land?

Either way, your creation has already served its purpose—an offering of mindfulness, made in harmony with the earth and ready to return to it.

Reflect
How did it feel to create something that will eventually fade away? How can this practice help you embrace change and impermanence?

More
Take a photo or sketch before letting it go, capturing the moment without needing to keep the creation itself.

Chalk Drawings

Art doesn't have to be permanent to be meaningful. In this practice, you use natural clay or chalk to create drawings on stone surfaces, pavements, or other outdoor spaces. As time, rain, or wind washes them away, you embrace the beauty of impermanence.

 *Outcomes*
- Encourages mindfulness by focusing on the joy of creating rather than the need for permanence.
- Reinforces the principle of leaving no trace by using only natural, biodegradable materials.

 *Items*
Natural clay, soft chalk, or crushed rock pigments. Water to mix

Intention: "I use the earth's minerals to create, embracing the wisdom that all things fade."

 *Steps*

Head outside and look for natural clay or soft chalk in the environment—or bring along a bit of eco-friendly, non-toxic art material if needed. Add just a little water and mix it with your fingers until it forms a smooth, paintable paste. Now find your canvas—a large stone, a patch of pavement, or another surface where your artwork will show up but won't leave a lasting mark. This is all about creating something beautiful that the earth can gently reclaim.

Use your fingers, a stick, a feather, or a leaf as your brush. Let your hand move freely—create patterns, symbols, shapes, or whatever wants to emerge. There's no need to plan it out. Just be with the feeling of the clay beneath your fingers, the coolness, the movement, the connection.

Focus on the process more than the result. This is about expressing yourself, not making something perfect. Let the rhythm of your hand and the softness of the earth guide you.

When you're finished, step back and take a moment to enjoy what you've created. And then, let it go. The rain will fall, the breeze will blow, and your artwork will slowly fade—becoming part of the land once more. It's a gentle reminder: art doesn't always need to last forever to be meaningful. Sometimes, its beauty is in the way it disappears.

 *Reflect*
How did it feel to create art knowing it would disappear? How does this practice mirror the natural cycles of change and renewal in life?

 *More*
Try creating different forms of nature-based chalk art in various seasons.

Flower Petal Collage

Nature's beauty is ever-changing, and this practice celebrates its fleeting artistry. Using fallen petals, you create a delicate, impermanent collage on the ground, forming shapes, patterns, or abstract designs that will eventually return to the earth.

- Encourages mindfulness and creative expression through natural materials.
- Reinforces the concept of impermanence and non-attachment.

Fallen flower petals
A flat surface such as soil, sand, grass, or stone

Intention: "I honour the fragility of petals, before the wind carries them away."

Take a slow, mindful walk through a garden, park, or natural space. As you wander, keep an eye out for fallen flower petals. Let yourself be guided by curiosity, choosing petals in different shapes, hues, and textures. Gently gather them, remembering to leave living flowers untouched so their beauty can continue to bloom.

When your hands feel full, find a quiet, undisturbed place where you can sit and begin your creation. A flat rock, a patch of grass, or a sandy spot will do perfectly. Start arranging your petals into a collage—maybe a spiral, a heart, a sunrise, or something completely abstract. Let your hands and heart guide the pattern, without overthinking.

As you place each petal, notice how the colours dance together, how the textures contrast or blend. Feel into the joy of creating something purely for this moment. When your design feels finished, sit with it for a while. Let your eyes take it in. Maybe snap a quick photo or make a sketch if you'd like to remember it later—but know that the real treasure is the experience itself.

When it's time to go, leave your collage where it is. Let the breeze scatter the petals, or the rain return them to the soil. Trust that nature knows how to hold what you've offered. This practice is your gentle reminder that beauty doesn't need to last forever to matter.

How did it feel to create something knowing it would soon disappear? How does this practice mirror the natural cycles of life and change?

You might also create a short poem or reflection inspired by your collage before letting nature take it back.

Nature Shadow Art

Light and shadow are nature's way of painting the world in motion. In this practice, you use natural objects like leaves, branches, or stones to create shadow designs on the ground. As the sun moves, your artwork transforms, reminding you of the beauty of impermanence.

 **Outcomes**
- Encourages observation of nature's rhythms and the passage of time.
- Fosters creativity using ephemeral elements like light and shadow.

 **Items**
Natural objects such as leaves, twigs, stones, or flowers.

Intention: "I embrace that some of the most beautiful things exist only for a moment."

 **Steps**

Find a spot where the sun casts strong, clear shadows—maybe in the morning or late afternoon when the light is low and golden. Look for a patch of open ground, a flat rock, or even a garden path. Start gathering natural objects that catch your eye—leaves, twigs, seedpods, feathers, or anything with interesting shapes. As you collect, notice how the light already plays through and around them.

Begin to arrange your objects on the ground in patterns or gentle designs, letting the shadows they cast become part of the artwork. You might notice delicate outlines, overlapping shapes, or long, stretching silhouettes. The shadow itself is your medium—alive, shifting, and full of quiet movement. Take a few slow breaths and really be with what's unfolding. Watch how the shadows lengthen or soften as the sun moves across the sky. Notice the contrast of light and dark, the way your creation is always becoming something new.

Stay for a while, simply observing. Let yourself be present with the impermanence—the dance of sun and shape, here only for a moment. When you're ready to move on, leave your materials where they are or gently return them to the land. This is art made of presence, of sunlight, and of change—and it doesn't need to last to leave a mark on your heart.

 **Reflect**
How did watching the shadows shift influence your sense of time and presence? How does this practice reflect the idea of impermanence in both art and life?

 **More**
You might also create shadow art using your own body, experimenting with different poses to interact with the natural world.

A Moment of Reflection

Before moving forward, take a moment to reflect on your experience with impermanence and the practice of creating without holding on.

How did it feel to create something knowing it would fade, wash away, or return to the earth? Did you notice any resistance or freedom in letting go?
___
___
___

What did these practices teach you about impermanence? How do you feel about the idea that beauty, like all things in life, is temporary?
___
___
___

How did nature respond to your offerings? Did you notice how the wind, rain, or time naturally transformed your art back into the landscape?
___
___
___

How might this practice of non-attachment apply to your daily life? Are there things—ideas, emotions, expectations—you are ready to let go of?
___
___
___

Do you feel ready to move forward? The next chapter explores the sacredness of nature and the self, inviting you to deepen your reverence and connection. Does this feel like a natural next step?

Take your time. Trust the ebb and flow of creation, knowing that nothing is ever truly lost—it simply changes form.

Chapter 8:
Sacred Earth, Sacred Self

Under ancient boughs and whispering winds,
you stand, rooted in the heartbeat of the land.
Each stone and blade of grass sings a timeless hymn—
a gentle chorus of renewal and enduring grace.

In the quiet blush of dawn and the soft sigh of dusk,
the earth cradles your spirit with tender care,
reminding you that every breath is a sacred gift.

Here, in the communion of nature and self,
you discover that you are both soil and seed,
a living reflection of the earth's ancient wisdom.

In this moment, as the world unfolds in gentle wonder,
your spirit and the land merge into one—
woven together by the sacred thread of life's eternal embrace.

Sacred Earth, Sacred Self

We often think of ourselves as separate from the world around us—a body walking through time with a mind that feels disconnected from the vastness of nature. Yet the more we look closely, the more we realise that we are intimately tied to the earth, to the elements, and to the flow of life itself. Our bodies are made of the same elements as the soil, the air, the water, and the stars. We breathe the same oxygen that flows through trees and forests, our hearts beat with the rhythm of life that pulses through every living being. In many ways we are nature, not separate from it.

The truth is, we are not just our physical bodies. The body is a temporary vessel constantly changing, always in motion, never fixed. Every cell within us is born, grows, and eventually fades, just like the leaves on a tree or the waves on the ocean. This impermanence is not something to fear, but rather, it is a sacred part of the cycle of life, a reminder that everything is in a constant state of transformation.

Our connection with nature is not just an abstract idea; it is a lived experience. When we pause and tune in, we can feel the pulse of life coursing through us—through our breath, through our senses, through the very energy that flows within and around us. In nature, we see that everything is interconnected. The earth provides the sustenance that keeps us alive, the sun gives us warmth and light, the rivers carry the water that nourishes our bodies. In this way, the earth itself is sacred—not just as a resource, but as a living, breathing entity that shares its essence with us.

Sacred Earth in Ancient Wisdom

Nature is the original temple, the first sanctuary. Long before humans built places of worship, they stood in awe beneath the vast sky, listened to the voice of the wind, and knelt before rivers and mountains with reverence. Land, sky, rivers, stones, fire, and trees were not just natural features, but living expressions of spirit. To walk through the forest was to walk through a temple. To sit beside a stream was to sit with a teacher. The sacred was not found in distant heavens—it was underfoot and in the breeze. In Indigenous Australian cultures, *Country* is alive. It holds stories, ancestors, spirit. It is not something you visit or use—it is part of who you are. The earth is family, memory, guide, and mirror. Respect for the land is not taught through rules—it is lived, through deep relationship and listening. Every action is a gesture of care and reverence.

In Vedic and yogic traditions, the five great elements—earth (*prithvi*), water (*apas*), fire (*agni*), air (*vayu*), and space (*akasha*)—are seen as both the building blocks of the universe and the building blocks of *you*. These elements are honoured in daily rituals, meditations, and practices that keep the inner and outer worlds in balance. The body is viewed as a sacred vessel, and nature as a divine reflection.

In Celtic and animistic traditions, groves were holy places, trees were keepers of wisdom, and the seasons marked sacred time. Offerings were made to rivers and stones, and the veil between earth and spirit was seen as thin, always shifting. The sacred was everywhere, and nothing was too ordinary to hold it.

These traditions share a knowing that modern life has often forgotten: that when we honour the earth as sacred, we begin to treat ourselves—and each other—with the same reverence. That to bow to the sun or the sea is to bow to the same force that animates your own heart.

Sacred Self

The sacred self is not something we can search for outside of us—it's always within, waiting to be noticed. It's easy to forget this in the busyness of life, but when we slow down and turn inward, we begin to sense it—the quiet, steady presence that has been with us all along. This essence, this true self, is not defined by our roles, our accomplishments, or our stories. It's the part of us that remains untouched by the passing moments, the part that knows peace even when the world around us feels chaotic.

When we take the time to truly attune to this inner being, we start to feel a deep sense of belonging to ourselves. It's like the calm in the centre of a storm—a stillness that doesn't need to prove anything, just is. It's the part of us that connects with the world around us from a place of authenticity, free from the need to seek validation or approval. This Self is whole, not because it has everything figured out, but because it embraces all of who we are—our light and our shadow, our joys and our struggles.

Sacred Self in Ancient Wisdoms

Throughout history, various wisdom traditions have explored the concept of the self or soul, offering profound insights into the nature of who we truly are. These teachings often emphasise that the self is not merely the body or the mind, but something deeper, eternal, and interconnected with the divine. In Vedantic and yogic teachings, this Self is called the Atman—the inner soul, untouched by suffering or change. It is not separate from the divine (Brahman), but an expression of it. Practices such as meditation, breathwork, mantra, and self-inquiry are used to peel back the layers of identity and thought, revealing the quiet truth of who we really are: not just a body, not just a mind, but a sacred presence.

In Buddhism, although the self is seen as impermanent and ever-changing, there is still a recognition of Buddha-nature—the awakened essence that exists within all beings. This is our capacity for compassion, wisdom, and peace, not something we must earn, but something we remember. Mindfulness and loving-kindness practices help cultivate awareness of this inherent purity.

In Indigenous traditions around the world, the sacred self is not separate from the land, ancestors, or community. Identity is shaped through deep relationship with nature, with story, and with spirit. The self is not seen as an isolated individual, but as part of a living web—a thread in the great tapestry of life. To honour oneself is to honour the earth, and vice versa.

As you explore the concept of the soul or spirit, remember that you don't have to define it according to any one religion or belief system. As human beings, we are uniquely gifted with the ability to choose what resonates most deeply within us. There is no single "right" way to understand our essence—what matters is what makes your heart sing, what brings you a sense of peace, purpose, and connection. All paths, no matter how different they may seem, lead to the same destination: a deeper understanding of who we are and our place in the world. Choose the path that feels most aligned with your heart, while remaining open to the truth that others may find meaning in different ways. Every journey is personal, and while your beliefs may differ from those around you, it's important to stay open, curious, and compassionate—embracing the diversity of paths that others follow, free from judgment. Through this openness, we deepen our understanding of ourselves and one another.

Why the Sages Went to the Forest

Since ancient times, sages, rishis, and mystics have gone into nature not to escape the world, but to come home to truth. In the forests, on mountain peaks, beside sacred rivers, they found what the noise of the world could not offer—stillness, clarity, and the deep remembrance of who they truly were. They understood what many of us are only beginning to remember: that the earth is not just beautiful, it is *sacred*.

Nature was their teacher. The quiet of the forest helped still the mind. The sunrise reminded them of life's cycles and continual renewal. The rivers spoke of flow, of letting go. And the open sky offered space—space to breathe, to witness, to expand. These wise beings didn't need textbooks or temples; they sat with the trees, the wind, the stars. And in that stillness, they listened.

On your *Wild Stillness* journey, you are walking a similar path—one not of withdrawal, but of return. You are invited to meet the land with reverence, to see yourself *not separate from* but *woven into* the fabric of nature. Just as the rishis knew the elements of the world were the same as the elements within, you too can experience your breath in the wind, your fire in the sun, your body in the earth, and your spirit in the sky.

Connecting with the Sacred

To feel the sacredness of the earth—and of your own self—is not a concept to be grasped with the mind. It is a slow unfolding, a quiet remembering that grows from within. It cannot be forced, and it cannot be rushed. That's why this chapter comes near the end of your *Wild Stillness* journey. The practices that have come before—presence, breath, heart, senses, expression—have been gently preparing the ground. Softening you. Rooting you. Opening space for this deeper kind of knowing to emerge.

To experience the sacred is not always dramatic. It often arrives in the smallest of moments: a sense of stillness as you sit beneath a tree, a warmth in your chest as you watch the sunrise, the sudden clarity that you are part of something vast and beautiful. These moments come when we are ready—not when we strive, but when we soften.

You might wonder, *How will I know if I'm making progress?* There is no measure, no test. But there are quiet signs.

Pay attention to your heart.
Are you becoming more gentle with yourself?
More compassionate with others?
Are you seeing beauty where you didn't before?
Are you pausing more often, listening more deeply, feeling more connected to the living world around you?

These are not small things. They are signs that something within you is shifting—that the sacred is not just something you're seeking, but something you're starting to *embody*. When your actions reflect kindness, love, forgiveness, patience… when you move through the world with reverence, even in simple ways… that is the sacred becoming alive in you.

Let it take time. Trust the pace of your own unfolding. Just as a flower doesn't rush to bloom, your connection with the sacred will deepen naturally, in its own season. All that's needed is your continued presence, your openness, and your willingness to return again and again to the stillness within.

Guided Meditation: Sacred Earth, Sacred Self

Find a comfortable, quiet space where you can sit or lie down, free from distractions. Allow yourself to settle into the present moment, closing your eyes gently. Take a deep breath in, and as you exhale, let go of any tension in your body. Feel your body begin to relax and soften. Begin by bringing your attention to your breath. Notice the gentle rise and fall of your chest or abdomen with each inhale and exhale. Allow your breath to become your anchor, grounding you in the present moment.

Inhale deeply… Exhale fully… Inhale peace… Exhale tension…

Now, bring your awareness to the earth beneath you. Feel the solid, supportive ground holding you. Imagine that you are connected to the earth, like the roots of a tree reaching deep into the soil. With each breath, feel yourself becoming more grounded, more connected to the earth beneath you. With every inhale, feel the earth's energy rising up through your body, nourishing and supporting you. With every exhale, let go of any tension or heaviness, releasing it back into the earth.

Begin to visualise the elements of nature around you. Picture the warmth of the sun above you, the cool breeze brushing your skin, the grounding strength of the earth below you, and the vastness of the sky above. Feel the air moving gently around you, refreshing and alive. Feel the earth beneath you, steady and eternal. Know that you are part of this great cycle—just as the sun shines, the wind blows, the earth nourishes, you too are a part of this rhythm, this dance of life.

Bring your awareness to the energy within your body. Imagine the energy of nature flowing through you, just as the wind moves through the trees, the water flows through the river, and the fire sparks in the hearth. Feel this energy vibrating through your cells, alive, expansive, and infinite. Notice how this energy flows not just *through* your body, but *as* your body. Feel the earth's energy rising through your feet, moving up through your legs, your torso, your arms, and your head. Feel this energy expanding outward, connecting you to everything around you—the earth, the sky, the trees, the wind, the stars.

Take a moment to reflect on this question: "If I am made of the same elements as the earth, the air, the water, the fire, and the stars—am I not, in some way, the same as these things? Am I too a part of this sacred dance?"

Allow yourself to feel a deep sense of unity with everything around you. You are not separate from the earth; you are not separate from the trees or the rivers or the sky. You are one with the vast, sacred web of life. Feel this connection flowing through you, alive in every cell, in every breath.

Imagine that your body is not just a physical form, but a vessel for this sacred energy. You are not only the body you see, but the energy that moves within it. You are not limited by your physical form, but part of the eternal flow of life, constantly changing, growing, evolving. As you sit here, fully present, feel the divine energy of the universe flowing through you, just as it flows through everything in nature.

Feel the infinite connection to all that is—earth, sky, stars, and spirit. Take a few moments to sit with this feeling. Feel the sacredness of your being, the sacredness of the earth, and the sacredness of all life. Let this realisation fill your heart and mind.

When you feel ready, slowly begin to bring your awareness back to the room around you. Feel the surface beneath you again. Notice the sounds, the light, and the space around you.

Take a deep breath in…and exhale fully, bringing this awareness of your sacredness with you. You are the earth, the sky, the stars, and the breath of life. You are sacred, and you are one with all that is.

Sacred Heart Altar

A natural altar is a sacred space—an offering to the land, a reflection of the beauty around you, and a place to pause in gratitude. In this practice, you gather elements from nature that speak to you, arranging them with care to honour the earth and your connection to it.

 *Outcomes*
- Cultivates reverence for the natural world through mindful gathering and arranging.
- Encourages gratitude by creating a space to honour the gifts of the earth.

 *Items*
A few natural treasures (such as a smooth stone, a feather, a sprig of wild herbs, or any items that call to you)

Intention: "I create this altar as a reflection of my heart's connection to nature."

 *Steps*

Take a slow, thoughtful walk through your favourite natural space. Let your gaze soften and notice what the earth has offered up—perhaps a fallen feather, a smooth stone, a curled leaf, or a sprig of dried herbs. Choose only what's already been released by nature, gathering a few pieces that speak to something within you.

When you feel ready, find a peaceful spot where your altar can sit undisturbed—a flat rock, a hollow in the roots of a tree, or a soft patch of moss. Begin arranging your items slowly, letting your hands move with care. You might create a circle, a spiral, or something entirely intuitive. There's no right way—just what feels meaningful to you.

Once your altar is complete, sit beside it for a while. Take a few deep breaths and feel the stillness. Let yourself absorb the energy of what you've created. You might offer a quiet word of thanks to the land, or simply rest in the connection.

If you like, set an intention for your altar. It could be for healing, inspiration, clarity, or simply to honour your relationship with nature. This altar can be a place you return to—a small sacred space woven between you and the land. Add to it gently over time, or allow the wind and rain to carry it back into the earth.

 *Reflect*
How did creating your altar help you feel connected to nature and your inner self?
What meanings or emotions did each natural element evoke for you?

 *More*
Revisit your sacred space regularly, adding or rearranging items as your feelings and insights evolve.

Sacred Sunrise Greeting

Each sunrise is a quiet miracle—earth turning, light returning, and the sky opening in radiant colour. In this practice, you greet the morning not as a routine, but as a sacred meeting between your inner self and the sun—the life-giving force that sustains all things.

 **Outcomes**
- Fosters gratitude for the sun's role in sustaining all living things.
- Awakens a deeper awareness of personal inner light and spiritual connection.

 **Items**
A view of the horizon. Candle and matches.

Intention: "I honour the sun as the source of life and light, and I awaken the light within myself."

 **Steps**

Rise before the sun and find a quiet place to sit where you can see the horizon. Bring a small candle with you and something to safely light it. As the sky begins to brighten, settle into stillness. Take a few slow, deep breaths. With each inhale, draw in the peace of early morning. With each exhale, let go of the night, clearing space within.

As the first light touches the earth, gently light your candle. Let this small flame symbolise your gratitude for the sun's gift—the warmth, the growth, the movement of weather, the cycles of time. Feel your connection to every plant that turns toward it, every drop of rain that it lifts from the oceans, every living thing it sustains.

Now turn inward. As you watch the sun rise, see the flame of your candle as a reflection of your own inner light—your awareness, your spirit, your potential to grow and shine. Feel the resonance between the great light in the sky and the quiet flame within your being. One lights the world; the other lights the way within.

Stay with this moment. Breathe. Offer a silent blessing or intention for the day ahead. You might simply whisper: "I am light. I am life. I am here." When the sun is fully risen or your time feels complete, gently blow out your candle sealing your intention.

 **Reflect**
In what ways do you feel the sun's presence in your daily life? How can you keep your own inner light nourished and shining? What is one way you can share light with others today?

 **More**
Take a mindful walk in the morning light, letting the energy of the sunrise further inspire your connection.

Tree Spirit Meditation

Trees are silent witnesses to time, standing with deep roots and open branches, offering wisdom through their quiet presence. In this practice, you sit beneath a tree and tune into its energy, imagining it as a wise teacher, and allow yourself to receive any insights or feelings.

 *Outcomes*
- Cultivates mindfulness by bringing full presence to the experience of sitting with a tree.
- Encourages a deeper sense of connection with nature's wisdom and stability.

 *Items*
A quiet outdoor space with a strong tree

Intention: "I sit with the trees and allow their quiet wisdom to remind me of my own inner strength."

 *Steps*

Find a tree that calls to you—not just any tree, but one that feels wise, grounded, and full of presence. Maybe it's one you've passed before, or maybe it's new to you. Let your feet guide you, and when you find it, settle beneath its branches. Sit close, or lean your back against its trunk. Feel the solidness behind you. Close your eyes and take a few slow, grounding breaths. Let yourself arrive fully. Notice the scent of the earth, the whisper of the breeze through the leaves, the texture of bark beneath your fingers.

Now, gently open your awareness to the spirit of the tree. Feel its presence, its living essence. Imagine it breathing with you—its slow, ancient rhythm syncing with your own. Feel its roots deep in the soil, and let your energy settle just as deeply. You might sense a quiet message rising through your spine, or a soft knowing settling in your heart. You don't need to speak aloud—your presence is enough. But if you feel called, offer a silent prayer, a word of thanks, or simply rest in the shared stillness.

Stay as long as you like, letting the tree hold you, just as it holds birds, wind, and time itself. When it feels complete, open your eyes slowly and return with reverence—carrying the calm strength of your rooted companion within you.

 *Reflect*
How did connecting with the tree's energy influence your sense of inner peace?
What insights or emotions surfaced as you listened to the tree's silent wisdom?

 *More*
Revisit this practice regularly with different trees, observing how each one offers unique wisdom and connection.

Water Blessing

Water is life—flowing, cleansing, and ever-changing. Approach a natural body of water with reverence, offering gratitude for its presence and the way it sustains all beings. This ceremony serves as a mindful act of appreciation of water's sacred role in our lives.

- Cultivates gratitude and reverence for water as a vital, sacred element.
- Encourages mindfulness by focusing on the sensation and movement of water.

A flowing stream, lake, river, or ocean.

Intention: "I honour the sacredness of water, offering gratitude for its life-giving energy."

Steps

Seek out a body of water that calls to you—perhaps a quiet stream, a still pond, or the gentle edge of the ocean. Let your heart guide you toward the place that feels most alive to your spirit. As you approach, begin to slow down. Soften your steps. Pause and simply witness—how the water moves, how it reflects the sky, how it responds to wind and light.

When you're ready, kneel or sit near the water. Dip your hands or feet gently into it. Close your eyes and feel—its temperature, its movement, its presence. Take a slow, full breath and remember: you are water, too. Flowing through your blood, your cells, your breath. The same element that fills rivers and rains also flows within you. There is no separation here.

Let that awareness rise through your body like a quiet tide—recognising that this water outside you is not other, but kin. Offer a silent word of gratitude for its life-giving force. For its wisdom, its patience, its power to cleanse and carry. If you wish, offer a small blessing—a whispered intention, a moment of heartfelt stillness, or a gentle touch upon the surface.

Sit with the water for a while, letting your own inner waters attune to its rhythm. Let it teach you about flow, surrender, and renewal. Feel the sacredness of this meeting—between body and earth, between inner and outer worlds. When you feel ready, rise slowly. Leave nothing behind but your reverence.

What aspects of water's movement, stillness, or energy resonated with you the most?
How can you honour and protect the water sources in your own life?

Return to this practice at different times of the year, noticing how the water changes.

Sacred Earth Meditation

The earth is an ancient, living entity, full of strength, wisdom, and grounding energy. In this meditation, you connect with the land beneath you, feeling its energy flow up through your body. This practice invites you to become one with the land, deeply rooted and at peace.

 *Outcomes*
- Cultivates grounding and presence by connecting with the earth's energy.
- Encourages mindfulness and deep relaxation through body awareness.

 *Items*
A quiet outdoor space with soft earth or grass to lie on.

Intention: "I connect with the steady presence of the earth, grounding me in strength and belonging."

 *Steps*

Find a quiet patch of land where you feel held by nature—somewhere soft with grass, warm stone, or cool soil beneath you. When you're ready, lie down and stretch out fully, allowing your body to rest completely against the earth. Close your eyes and begin to breathe slowly and deeply. With each exhale, feel your weight sinking a little more. There's nothing to hold up. The earth is holding you now.

As you settle, begin to sense the ground beneath you—not just as something solid, but as something alive. This is the same earth that grew the trees, shaped the mountains, cradled the oceans. And it's the same earth that shaped you. Your bones, your blood, your organs—all made from its elements. Earth becoming human. You are not separate from this ground. You are made of it.

With each inhale, imagine the ancient energy of the land rising into you—steadiness, wisdom, calm. Let it fill your body like rich soil fills roots. With each exhale, release anything you no longer need—tension, worry, old stories. Let it fall into the earth, where it can be held and transformed. Rest here for a while, feeling the quiet truth of belonging. You are of the earth. And right now—you are simply here. Alive. Connected. Held. When you feel ready, gently begin to return to the surface of things. Wiggle your fingers and toes. Roll onto your side. Sit up slowly, bringing the calm strength of the earth with you.

 *Reflect*
How did lying on the earth affect your sense of presence and connection?
What sensations or images arose as you visualised becoming one with the land?

 *More*
Try this meditation in different landscapes.

Sacred Nature Walk

Nature is filled with quiet wonders, waiting to be noticed. Take a slow, mindful walk in a natural space that feels meaningful to you. With each step, you shift your awareness to the small details honouring the sacred connection between yourself and the living world.

- Deepens your connection with nature by fostering gratitude and presence.
- Encourages mindfulness through slow, intentional movement and observation.

A quiet natural space that feels special to you

Intention: "I walk with reverence, seeing the land not just as scenery, but as a sacred teacher and guide."

Begin by finding a natural place that feels meaningful to you. Somewhere you can walk slowly, without hurry or expectation. As you begin, pause for a moment. Feel your feet on the ground. Take a deep breath. Let yourself arrive fully, like a leaf floating gently to the forest floor. Start to walk slowly. With each step, let your awareness widen. Notice the smallest things—a glint of dew, the way light filters through the branches. Let yourself be guided—not by your thoughts, but by a sense of quiet curiosity.

As you walk, gently offer silent thanks. And as you do, remember: this is not just the world around you. It is also the world within you. The minerals in the soil are in your bones. The water in the stream flows through your veins. The fire of the sun warms your breath. You are not a visitor here—you belong. Feel the sacred thread that runs through it all—through you, through tree, through sky. It's not something you need to create. It's already here.

Let your awareness expand into the space between things—the energy that connects leaf to branch, you to tree, breath to breeze. It is all sacred. You are sacred. Walk this path not as a task, but as a prayer. Let your body become a blessing. Let your presence be a quiet act of devotion to the living world that is also you. And when your walk draws to a close, pause once more. Place a hand on your heart. Feel the aliveness within you—the same aliveness that hums in the roots and the sky. Whisper thank you, and carry that stillness with you into whatever comes next.

What details stood out to you the most during your walk?
How did expressing gratitude shift your awareness or emotions?

After your walk, find a quiet place to sit and journal about your experience.

Moon Journal

Let the moon become your nightly companion, a quiet witness to your inner world. In this practice, you take a few moments each evening to pause and connect with the moon. Observing her shape, position, and light becomes a gentle ritual of presence.

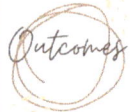 *Outcomes*
- Cultivates a sense of rhythm, emotional awareness, and inner attunement.
- Strengthens connection with the cosmos, nature's cycles, and the body's wisdom.

 *Items*
A view of the moon over a period of time (one month if possible)

Intention: "I honour the moon as a mirror of my own rhythms and find peace in her quiet presence."

 *Steps*

Each night step outside and take a quiet moment to meet the moon. Look up. Let your gaze soften. Where is the moon tonight? Is it rising, high in the sky, or just a sliver resting low on the horizon? What shape is she wearing—a full, glowing circle or the faint whisper of a crescent? Notice her colour, her light, and the way she makes you feel.

Take a deep breath and simply be with her. Let this be an intentional connection—not just looking, but feeling. This is not just light in the sky. This is the same moon that has guided tides, migrations, rituals, and reflections for generations. She sees you too. Feel her energy gently washing over you. Let it soften the day's worries, loosen what's tight, and carry away any heaviness you no longer need. Just like the tides, she has the power to move water—and since your body is made mostly of water, why wouldn't she stir something in you too?

Close your eyes for a moment and feel into your body. Can you sense the subtle pull? The calm? The mystery? The moon knows the language of rhythm, of release, of reflection. Let her remind you. Send her your gratitude—silently or aloud. Thank her for lighting the night, for her steady presence, for the gentle way she reflects the sun without needing to burn.

This is your sacred nightly pause. A soft remembering that you are not alone under this sky. You are part of something vast, ancient, and deeply connected.

 *Reflect*
Is there a part of you that feels full, or a part that is waning? What patterns or emotions have you noticed over the past few moon phases?

 *More*
Create a moon phases tracker in your journal and notice how your energy and emotions shift across the lunar cycle.

Elemental Offering

Earth. Air. Fire. Water. The four sacred elements are not just part of the world around us—they are within us. They are the language of the soul, the building blocks of all life, and ancient teachers of balance, presence, and transformation

- Deepens connection with nature through attunement to the elements.
- Encourages inner reflection through symbolic ritual.

A leaf or small stone, A feather or dried flower, A candle, or dried herb, A shell,, or bowl of water.

Intention: "I honour the elements—earth, air, fire, and water- and their presence within all things."

Find a quiet, undisturbed outdoor space where you can sit in stillness. Bring four small, symbolic offerings - one for each element. Close your eyes and take a few deep, slow breaths, inviting your body to arrive fully in this sacred moment. Open your ritual by silently or softly acknowledging the circle of life and your place within it.

Earth - Hold your leaf or stone and place it gently on the ground. Whisper a blessing of gratitude for the soil that holds us, the trees that root deeply, and the strength within your own body. Feel your bones and your breath sink deeper into presence. "Thank you, sacred Earth, for your stability, support, and nourishment. May I walk grounded and whole."

Air -Lift your feather or dried flower and raise it toward the sky. Feel the breeze on your skin, the breath in your lungs. Offer this token to the wind. Honour the power of breath, inspiration, and the unseen forces that guide change. "Thank you, sacred Air, for your clarity, movement, and insight. May I trust the winds of change and breathe with grace."

Fire - Hold your candle or herb to your heart before placing it on the ground or in a fire-safe dish. Light it if safe to do so, or simply visualise flame. Connect to your inner spark—the will to transform, to rise, to radiate. "Thank you, sacred Fire, for your warmth, your transformation, your passion. May I carry your light in all that I do."

Water - Gently touch your shell, flower, or water vessel. Pour a little water onto the ground or dip your fingers into it. Feel its cool flow, and reflect on the emotions, memories, and intuition it carries. "Thank you, sacred Water, for your flow, your healing, your wisdom. May I soften, surrender, and listen deeply."

Sit in silence, feeling the balance of the four elements all around and within you—body, breath, spirit, and soul. You may place all offerings in a small circle before you, or return them to nature with care.

Rainfall Blessing

Rain is more than water—it is the sky touching the earth, a sacred offering from the heavens. In many traditions, rain is seen as a blessing, a purifier, a divine rhythm that nourishes life and cleanses the soul. Walk into it with open arms and an open heart.

 *Outcomes*
- Encourages mindfulness by bringing full awareness to the sensory experience of rain.
- Strengthens connection to nature's rhythms by embracing rather than resisting the elements.

 *Items*
A rainy day.
Comfortable outdoor clothing (or the willingness to simply get wet

Intention: "I welcome the rain as a sacred gift, allowing it to cleanse my spirit."

 *Steps*

When the rain begins to fall, step outside into a space where you can be safely and mindfully present with it. Stand still for a moment, letting the rhythm of the rain meet your body. Take a slow, deep breath and feel the droplets touch your skin—cool, soft, awakening. Notice where they land: your face, your hands, your shoulders. Let your body receive them as sacred.

Open your arms gently to the sky, whispering a silent or spoken prayer of gratitude. Feel yourself not just in the rain, but of the rain—remembering that the same water flowing from the sky flows through your blood, your cells, your breath. If you feel moved to walk, do so slowly and mindfully. With each step, let the rain wash over your thoughts, your emotions, your burdens. Let it cleanse what no longer serves you.

You may speak a simple blessing:
"Bless me, Rain, that I may soften and grow. Wash me clean, that I may begin again."

When your time in the rain feels complete, take one last breath of the earthy, rain-soaked air. Offer your thanks to the sky, and return indoors slowly, wrapped in the sacredness of the moment.

 *Reflect*
How did it feel to embrace the rain instead of seeking shelter from it?
What emotions or thoughts surfaced as you experienced the rain with gratitude?

 *More*
Try this practice in different types of rain—gentle drizzles, summer storms, or misty showers—and notice how each experience feels unique.

Prayer Flags

For centuries cultures around the world have created **sacred flags to carry prayers, blessings, and dreams into the wind—whispers of spirit woven into the breath of nature**. Each flag becomes a sacred vessel, infused with heartfelt intentions, symbols of healing, or gratitude.

- Deepens spiritual connection through symbolic creation and sacred offering.
- Encourages intention-setting as a devotional practice.

Small pieces of biodegradable fabric or leaves. Natural paints, charcoal, or earth pigments. Cotton or string.

Intention: "I offer my prayers knowing they are heard, held, and carried on the breath of the world."

Begin by finding a peaceful, sacred space outdoors.. Take a few moments to connect with the land—place your hands on the earth, take a deep breath, and invite stillness into your body. Gather your materials: fallen leaves, soft bark, or squares of natural fabric (undyed cotton or linen work well). Also gather natural twine, thread, or a branch to string your flags together.

Hold each flag material in your hands for a moment. Close your eyes and silently ask: What blessing, what intention, what healing prayer wishes to be carried from me into the world? Using natural paints, ink, charcoal, or even pressed flowers, create a symbol, word, or simple image on each flag. Let it come intuitively—from the heart, not the mind. You might inscribe: peace, healing, courage, gratitude, or draw the sun, spiral, river, or seed.

As you work, speak softly to the wind: "May this prayer be heard. May it travel. May it bless."

When your flags are complete, tie them to a string, a branch, or weave them into a tree or garden space that feels sacred to you. Offer a few final words of thanks, then step back and let nature receive your offering. Over time, the elements—sun, rain, wind—will soften your prayer flags. This too is part of the blessing. They are not meant to last forever. They are meant to be carried.

What intention or message did you choose, and why?
How did it feel to create and release your blessing into nature?

Return to the same place after some time to see how nature has interacted with your prayer.

Silent Solitude

In the hush of the natural world, something sacred stirs. Beyond words, beyond thought, there is a presence—a quiet intelligence that lives in the trees, the stones, the wind. In this practice, you are invited to sit in reverent stillness with the earth.

- Strengthens self-awareness by creating space for inner stillness and reflection.
- Deepens your connection to the natural world as a sacred space for insight and renewal.

A quiet outdoor setting where you will be undisturbed

Intention: "I am deeply connected to all that is sacred."

Find a quiet place in nature that feels safe and inviting. Let your body be drawn to the space—it will know. Sit or lie down comfortably, allowing your body to rest fully on the earth. Take a few slow, grounding breaths, feeling your connection to the land beneath you.

Close your eyes or soften your gaze. Let all doing fall away. There is nowhere to go, nothing to achieve. Just be.

Begin to notice the sounds around you—the gentle movements of air, the call of a bird, the soft creak of branches. Let them pass through you like a breeze. Resist the urge to label or interpret. Simply receive.

If thoughts arise, gently let them go, returning your awareness to the stillness beneath the sound. Allow your breath to be natural, your body soft.

As you sit, you may feel the presence of the earth deepening—subtle shifts in temperature, movement, or emotion. Welcome them. Allow the land to meet you, to speak in its own silent way. Remain for as long as you feel called. When you feel complete, slowly bring your awareness back to your breath, then your body. Offer a silent word of thanks before rising gently and walking slowly back into the world.

How did the silence of nature affect your inner stillness? What did you notice in the absence of words and distractions?

Try this meditation in different places—by a river, beneath an ancient tree, in an open field—and notice how each landscape offers a unique presence.

Seasonal Celebration

Each season arrives with its own sacred invitation—an unseen hand guiding us through cycles of growth, letting go, rest, and renewal. By pausing to reflect, you attune yourself to nature's rhythms and the deeper currents of your own inner transformation.

- Encourages sacred ritual as a grounding and reflective practice.
- Deepens connection to the earth's seasonal energy and wisdom.

A quiet outdoor space in nature

Intention: "I honour the turning of the seasons as a mirror of my own change and sacred unfolding."

Choose a day near a seasonal turning point—the equinox, solstice, or any natural transition that speaks to you. Go for a slow, mindful walk in nature, letting your senses open. As you walk, gently collect a few natural items that reflect the essence of the season. A golden leaf, a pinecone, a fallen feather, a flower in bloom, a smooth stone warmed by the sun. Gather only what has fallen naturally and feel light in your hand. Let each piece feel chosen, not taken.

Find a quiet spot outdoors where you can sit and reflect. Take a few deep breaths and allow yourself to be fully present with the energy of this moment.

Ask yourself: - In spring, what is beginning within me?
- In summer, what is flourishing in my life?
- In autumn, what am I ready to release?
- In winter, where can I soften and go inward?

You may wish to write these reflections in your journal, whisper them aloud, or simply hold them in your heart. Offer a simple gesture of gratitude to the land—this could be a bow, a breath, or a moment of stillness. As you return home, place your gathered items on your personal altar or a special place in your home. Let this seasonal altar evolve through the year, reflecting not just what is happening around you, but what is awakening within.

What season are you in internally, and how does it mirror the outer world? Which object from nature spoke to you most, and why?

Revisit your seasonal spot in nature with each new turn of the wheel, refreshing your altar as you go.

Firelight Reflection

Fire has always been a sacred teacher—burning away what no longer serves, illuminating the darkness, and igniting the spark of renewal. The flames become a mirror, showing you what is ready to be released and what is longing to rise within you.

- Encourages introspection through the transformative symbolism of fire.
- Supports emotional and spiritual release in a grounded, natural setting.

A campfire, fireplace or candle

Intention: "I sit with the fire to let go, to illuminate, and to invite new energy into my life.""

Find a safe place to sit near a flame—this might be a campfire under the stars, a small outdoor firepit, or even a candlelit space indoors. Wherever you are, treat the fire as sacred. Begin by settling into stillness. Take a few deep breaths and feel your body soften with the warmth. Gaze gently at the flames—not with effort, but with openness. Let your awareness become calm.

As you watch the fire dance, bring to mind something within you that you are ready to release. It may be an old story, a fear, a habit, or a thought that weighs you down. Name it quietly to yourself.

Imagine placing that energy into the fire—not physically, but with your breath and intention. As the flames flicker and shift, allow them to transform what you've offered into light and ash.

Take a few moments to sit with the emptiness that remains—the clear space within. Then, if it feels right, bring your attention to what you wish to welcome: a new beginning, clarity, creativity, or strength. Let the fire's glow awaken this energy within you.

You may choose to speak your release and intention aloud, or simply hold it silently in your heart. Stay for as long as you feel called, letting the fire teach you through its warmth, movement, and mystery. Before you leave, whisper a simple word of thanks.

What did the fire show you or stir within you?
What felt ready to be released tonight?
What are you inviting in as you move forward?

Write what you wish to release on paper and safely burn it in the fire.

Nature Reading Ritual

Some words are meant to be read not just with the mind, but with the heart open to the hush of the earth. As the words mingle with birdsong, rustling leaves, and shifting light, their meaning deepens. You are not just reading—you are receiving.

 **Outcomes**
- Strengthens the felt sense of unity between language, land, and self.
- Cultivates reverence through mindful stillness and multisensory awareness.

 **Items**
sacred text, chapter openers or a meaningful passage

Intention: "I read with my whole being—heart open to the land, and words rooted in soul."

 **Steps**

Choose a piece of writing that holds personal or spiritual meaning for you. This might be a sacred text, a passage from an eco-spiritual author, or one of the poetic chapter openers from this book. Head outdoors with your chosen words and find a quiet, undisturbed place to sit. It could be under a tree, beside a stream, on a rocky outcrop, or anywhere that feels gently alive.

Settle in and take a few slow breaths. Before reading, let your senses attune to the space around you. Feel the breeze, listen to the birds or distant hum, observe the textures of the land. Let nature become part of the experience.

Begin to read slowly—aloud or silently—letting each word land softly. Between passages or stanzas, pause. Don't rush to understand. Instead, feel. Let the meaning unfold in the space between you and the earth.

Notice what phrases echo in your heart, what lines stir something ancient in you. Let the natural world respond with its own language—the rustle of a leaf, the call of a bird, the warmth of sun on skin.

When you finish, place the text gently in your lap or beside you. Close your eyes for a moment and rest in stillness, letting the experience settle within.

 **Reflect**
How did the natural world shift the meaning or feeling of the text? What stayed with you most—was it a line, a sound, a sensation??

 **More**
Create a small reading altar in nature with a candle, flower, or stone.

Stargazing Reverie

The stars have long been seen as messengers of the divine—guiding, illuminating, reminding us that we are never truly separate from the greater whole. The vastness above is not distant—it is a reflection of what lives within you.

- Encourages reflection on your place within the interconnected web of life.
- Cultivates gratitude for the guiding lights —both celestial and within.

Somewhere you can sit or lay down to view the stars.

Intention: "I remember that I am not separate—I am part of the stars, the earth, and the sacred whole."

Choose a clear night when the stars are visible and find a place outdoors with an open view of the sky. Bring a blanket or mat so you can lie back comfortably. Settle into stillness. Take a few deep, grounding breaths and soften your gaze toward the sky. Allow yourself to simply receive the light—tiny flickers across the endless dark.

Notice how your breath slows in the quiet. Feel the pulse of your body, steady and alive beneath the vastness. Let the stars remind you that you are not small—you are part of this magnificence. You are held in it.

Let your thoughts drift gently, not to problem-solve, but to wonder: Where did I come from? What lights have guided me? What do I carry within me that is eternal? The vastness above is not distant—it is a reflection of what lives within you. As you gaze into the stars, remember: you are stardust, woven from the same light, part of the same sacred story.

If you feel moved, speak a silent prayer of thanks—to the cosmos, to the earth, to the unseen rhythm that holds it all together. Or simply whisper, "I am part of this."

Stay as long as you wish, letting the stars fill your awareness. When you feel ready to return, carry that connection back with you like a thread of light in your heart.

Did you feel a sense of belonging to something larger? How might you live more fully from the awareness that we are all connected?

Keep a stargazing journal where you write down insights or dreams sparked by the night sky.

Sunset Reflection

The setting sun marks the gentle close of another day—a reminder that endings hold their own beauty and wisdom. In this practice, you sit in stillness as the sky shifts in colour, letting the transition from light to darkness be a time of reflection and peace.

Outcomes
- Encourages mindfulness by attuning to the transition from day to night.
- Fosters gratitude and reflection on the experiences of the day.

Items
A quiet outdoor space with an open view of the sunset.

Intention: "I pause in gratitude for the day's gifts, releasing all that no longer serves me."

Steps

Find a quiet place where you can sit and watch the sun's descent. Let this be a sacred pause—an invitation to step out of the rhythm of doing and into the quiet unfolding of the day's end. Take a few deep breaths and gently let go of any weight you've been carrying. Allow the soft light to wash over you as the sun lowers toward the horizon.

As the sky begins to shift, reflect gently on your day. What did this light reveal to you? What moments stood out? What feelings surfaced? Let the sun's glow guide your awareness to the places in you that are growing, changing, or asking to be seen.

Offer quiet gratitude—for the people, the lessons, the beauty, and even the challenges. Honour it all. The light of the day has shown you what needed your attention. And now, it asks you to surrender. As the colours begin to fade, allow yourself to release. Let go of what no longer serves, of what is complete. Trust the darkening sky—it too is sacred. With every breath, soften into the mystery of nightfall. This is a time for rest, renewal, and unseen transformation.

Sit in stillness as the last light slips below the horizon. Feel yourself held in this in-between—between light and dark, between what has been and what will become. Let it be enough simply to be here, gently dissolving into the great rhythm of the earth's turning.

Reflect
How did watching the sunset change your perspective on endings?
What is one thing you can release as the day closes, making space for new beginnings tomorrow?

More
Return to the same place regularly, deepening your connection with the land and its rhythms.

A Moment of Reflection

Before stepping into the next chapter, take a moment to reflect on your journey of recognising the sacred—within nature and within yourself.

How has your understanding of sacredness evolved? Did you experience moments in nature where you felt a deep sense of connection or reverence?

_____
_____
_____

Did you notice a shift in how you see yourself in relation to the earth? How does recognising yourself as part of nature—not separate from it—change the way you move through the world?

_____
_____
_____

How did it feel to honour the elements—earth, air, fire, and water—as part of yourself? Did any particular element resonate more deeply with you?

_____
_____
_____

Did you experience any resistance in seeing yourself as sacred? What might help you soften into a deeper sense of self-honour and belonging?

_____
_____
_____

Do you feel ready to move forward? The next chapter invites you to give back to the earth—not as an obligation, but as an act of love and gratitude. Does this feel like a natural next step?

Take your time. Allow the sacred to unfold in its own way, in its own time. Trust that this connection is always present—within you, around you, and in every step you take upon the earth.

Chapter 9:
Giving Back to the Earth

I have walked this land with open hands,
listening to the whispers of the trees,
the quiet breath of the river,
the heartbeat of the hills beneath my feet.

I have sat in stillness,
letting the wind weave through my ribs,
the sun paint warmth upon my skin,
the stars remind me that I, too, am made of light.

Now, the time has come to give back.
Not from duty, not from debt,
but from the love that has grown in my chest—
wild, untamed, endless.

This is not the end of the journey,
but the beginning of a promise—
to walk as kin to the land,
to live as if the earth is sacred,
because it always has been.

Giving Back to the Earth

You have slowed down, listened deeply, breathed with the trees, opened your heart, awakened your senses, created, expressed, and honoured the sacred within and around you. Along the way, nature has offered you her quiet wisdom, beauty, stillness, and healing. And now—your heart full, your spirit softened—you arrive at a natural turning point: the desire to give something *back*.

When we are deeply nourished by something, it's natural to respond with gratitude. Giving back to the earth is not a rule or obligation—it is a *joyful response* to love. It arises not from guilt, but from reverence. It is the heart's way of saying, "Thank you."

We, as humans, are uniquely blessed with the consciousness to choose our actions. Unlike any other sentient being, we have the ability to decide whether we tread lightly or with harm, whether we contribute or consume, whether we live in harmony or separation. This awareness is a gift. And when we choose to give back—not from guilt, but from love—we complete the circle.

This chapter is about exploring simple, meaningful ways to live in reciprocity with nature. You don't need to change the world. You only need to begin—with small actions, with presence, with love. Whether it's tending a garden with care, picking up litter from a trail, putting water out for wildlife, planting trees, or supporting conservation efforts, every act of care becomes part of the greater web of healing.

Involving Children in the Practice of Giving Back

Children are naturally curious, compassionate, and connected to the living world. When we invite them into the practice of giving back to the earth, we're not just teaching them about sustainability—we're helping them remember their belonging. We're planting seeds of reverence, responsibility, and joy that will grow with them for life.

As a teacher for over 30 years, I was always passionate about connecting children with nature—not only to support their learning, but to nourish their wellbeing and sense of belonging in the world. I saw again and again how real-life, hands-on experiences in nature grounded children, sparked their curiosity, and helped them feel calm, confident, and connected. I was always looking for ways to weave this into the school day— not just as a science topic or a sustainability unit, but as a way of being.

That's why this final chapter, Giving Back to the Earth, holds such meaning. It's a natural extension of everything children learn through presence, care, and wonder. When we offer them simple, heartfelt ways to give back—to tend a garden, clean up a green space, or create a gratitude ritual—they begin to understand that they are not separate from the earth, but a vital part of it. These practices aren't just good for the environment—they're good for the soul. They build empathy, responsibility, and joy. And when we do them together, as a class or school community, we nurture something even more powerful: a culture of care.

Simple Weekly Ways to Give Back – For Families and Schools

Incorporating earth-honouring actions into everyday life doesn't need to be complicated. Whether you're a parent, grandparent, teacher, or caregiver, small, regular gestures of care can help children build a lifelong relationship with the natural world. These practices become not only lessons—but memories. Here are some gentle ways to begin, one week at a time:

For Families

- Tree Time Tuesdays – Take a walk to visit a favourite tree. Sit beneath it, observe its leaves or bark, and give thanks. Let children name the tree and form a personal bond with it.
- Waste-Free Wednesdays – Dedicate one day a week to creating no waste in lunchboxes or meals. Involve children in choosing reusable containers and thinking about where rubbish goes.
- Weekend Wild Hours – Carve out 1-2 hours on the weekend for unstructured nature time—no agenda, no screens, just being outside and exploring with curiosity.
- Compost Sundays – Start a composting ritual together, adding scraps, stirring the pile, and noticing how the earth transforms what we no longer need.

For Schools

- Monday Garden Moment – Begin the week with a short time outside—watering plants, observing insects, or simply noticing the weather together.
- Wildlife Wednesdays – Invite students to learn about a native plant or animal each week and how they can help protect it. Create a shared poster or display.
- Nature Buddy System – Pair older and younger students for regular nature walks, litter clean-ups, or creating ephemeral art in the school yard.
- Seasonal Giving Projects – Each term, plan a bigger action—like planting trees, creating bee habitats, or hosting a "Green Day" celebration of nature.

A Gentle Beginning: Ways to Give Back

In the pages that follow, you'll find offerings—ideas and inspirations to help you begin giving back to the earth in ways that feel meaningful and real. This is not a checklist. It's simply a sharing of possibilities—a way to spark your heart, awaken your creativity, and help you discover how *you* might walk a little more gently, a little more lovingly, upon the earth.

Some of these suggestions can be done at home. Others may invite you into your local community, or even connect you to broader, global movements of care. All of them come from the same place: a wish to live in harmony with nature and to give something beautiful in return for all we receive—air, sunlight, water, nourishment, shade, beauty, life.

As you read through the suggestions, pause. Feel into your heart. Does one activity speak to you? Spark a memory? Stir your energy? Begin there. Let it be joyful. Let it be an offering—not from obligation, but from love. We don't need to do everything. We only need to do something, and to do it with care.

Giving Back... at Home

Mindful Water Use

Water is one of the earth's most precious gifts—essential, sacred, and often taken for granted. Begin to treat water with reverence in your daily life. Collect rainwater to nourish your plants. Turn taps off when not in use. Notice the sound of water as it flows, and say a quiet thank you. Whether you're washing dishes, showering, or standing beside a river, take a moment to honour this life-giving element. When we bless the water, we bless the source of all life.

Wild Garden Corner

Let a corner of your garden—or even a few pots on a balcony—go wild. Resist the urge to tidy, trim, or control. Allow native grasses, wildflowers, or fallen logs to become shelter for insects, birds, and small creatures. This small act creates a sanctuary of biodiversity and reminds you that nature thrives in the freedom to simply be. Watch it change with the seasons and feel the joy of coexisting rather than managing.

Pollinator Haven

Bees, butterflies, and other pollinators play a vital role in the health of our ecosystems, yet they're often overlooked. Plant a patch of nectar-rich flowers—lavender, bottlebrush, tea tree, grevillea, or native daisies—and watch your space hum with life. Even a few pots can make a difference. This simple gesture helps sustain entire food systems. You're not just planting flowers—you're planting life.

Earth-Friendly Cleaning

Our everyday choices ripple outward. Swap out harsh chemical cleaners for natural alternatives—vinegar, lemon, eucalyptus, bicarb. These gentle solutions clean effectively without harming water systems or soil. When we cleanse our homes without leaving harm in our wake, we honour both our inner and outer environment. It's a quiet form of devotion—caring for the home, the body, and the earth in one gentle sweep.

Indoor Nature Connection

Bring the living world into your home by growing herbs, indoor plants, or even a small native tree in a pot. Tend to them with care. Watch how they respond to light, water, and time. Let your home be a sanctuary not just for you, but for green life. This daily connection, even in the smallest pot, keeps your relationship with nature alive—especially on days you can't be outside.

Giving Back... at Home

Tend a Bird Bath

Water is a gift not just for us, but for the birds and animals who share our space. Place a shallow bowl or stone bird bath in your garden or balcony and keep it filled with clean water. On hot days, it may be life-saving. Watch the birds bathe, drink, and gather—bringing their song and presence into your world. This simple offering becomes a bridge between you and the wild, a gentle act of hospitality and care.

Plant Native Trees

Planting native trees is a deeply restorative act—for the land, for wildlife, and for the future. Choose trees that belong to your region, ones that naturally support the local ecosystem. As the tree grows, so too does your relationship with it. You may visit it, breathe with it, sit in its shade. Let it become a symbol of your commitment to nurture what sustains us all.

Composting Ritual

What we discard still holds value. Composting is a sacred practice of returning to the earth what once came from it—transforming waste into nourishment. Set up a compost system at home and notice how your awareness shifts. Scraps become offerings. Soil becomes rich and alive. Each banana peel or leaf becomes part of the great cycle of regeneration. Composting is a quiet way to honour the unseen life that sustains us.

Energy Awareness Day

Choose one day a week to live more simply, consciously reducing your use of electricity. Light candles as the sun sets. Let natural light guide your day. Minimise devices, and allow quiet and slowness to return. Notice how it feels in your body, your mind, your space. This practice is not about deprivation—it's about reconnecting with the natural rhythms that often go unnoticed. It's a way to say: I am willing to slow down for the sake of balance.

Sacred Earth Altar

Create a small space—a windowsill, a table, a corner of the garden—where you can place objects gathered with care: a feather, a stone, a leaf, a bowl of water. Let this altar be a place of reflection, intention, and gratitude. You may light a candle, say a blessing, or simply sit in silence. This sacred space becomes a visual reminder that the earth is not just beautiful, but worthy of reverence. Let your altar change with the seasons, and let your heart grow more connected each time you visit it.

Giving Back... Locally

Litter Clean-Up Walk

Walk through your local park, forest, or beach with a bag and gloves—not just as a clean-up, but as an act of reverence. Each piece of rubbish you remove is a way of saying thank you to the land for all it gives. As you walk, listen. Notice the beauty beneath the debris. This is not about perfection—it's about participation. Let your presence be a quiet offering of care.

Tree Guardianship

Choose a tree near your home—a street tree, a gum in your yard, or a favourite old friend in the park. Visit it often. Sit beneath it. Clear away litter or weeds from its roots. Notice how it changes with the seasons. Over time, your bond will deepen. You may begin to feel a sense of kinship, a silent exchange of breath and being. This tree becomes your teacher in rootedness, resilience, and stillness.

Community Nature Exchange

Connection thrives when it's shared. Organise or join a small gathering—a seed swap, a plant-sharing morning, or a storytelling circle where people share their experiences with nature. These events don't need to be big or formal—just honest and heart-led. They remind us that community is also part of the earth's ecology, and that connection to nature is something we can grow together.

Nature Gratitude Circle

Gather with a few friends or family members in a quiet outdoor space. Sit in a circle and take turns sharing: What has nature given you lately? How do you feel called to give back? This reflection, spoken aloud in the presence of the earth, can be a beautiful, grounding ritual. Let it be informal, heartfelt, and real. Gratitude shared becomes a seed of deeper care.

Native Plant Restoration

Look for local bushcare or land restoration groups working to regenerate native ecosystems. Join a planting day, help remove invasive species, or support the preservation of indigenous flora. Even just once a month, your presence makes a difference. As you place a native seedling into the ground, know that you're helping to restore the original story of the land—one that remembers balance, beauty, and belonging.

Giving Back... Locally

Library of Wild Knowledge

Books carry seeds of awareness. Donate nature-themed books—about ecology, native wildlife, plant wisdom, or conservation—to a local library, school, or community space. Whether it's a children's picture book about bees or a guide to bush regeneration, each book becomes a doorway for someone else to begin their own journey of connection. Sharing knowledge is one way we plant invisible forests.

Nature-Inspired Art Installations

Create a temporary artwork in a natural setting—using stones, twigs, fallen leaves, or petals. Choose a local park or quiet space where your creation can bring beauty and presence to others without leaving harm. Let it be an offering, a celebration of the land, a reminder of the wild stillness that lives all around. And then, let it return to the earth—just as everything eventually does.

Earth Gratitude Mural or Nature Journal Wall

Invite students to express their appreciation for nature through drawings, poems, or short reflections, then display them as a mural or rotating gallery in a shared school space. Parents can join in by contributing artwork or helping with display and organisation. This shared expression of gratitude helps cultivate a culture of care and reverence for the natural world—one voice, one leaf, one message at a time.

Recycled Paper & Seed Card Project

Organise a simple workshop where students make handmade paper using recycled materials and embed native seeds into the pulp. These seed cards can be gifted to the school community or planted in designated garden areas. As the paper dissolves and the seeds grow, students see a tangible reminder that even waste can give life—and that their creative efforts can bloom into something beautiful for the earth.

Nature Play Days

Encourage the school community to set aside regular times for Nature Play— open-ended, unstructured time outdoors where children (and even older students) can explore, create, and connect with the natural environment. Set up simple spaces with logs, rocks, sticks, mud kitchens, or natural materials and let imagination lead the way. These moments of play build deep relationships with the land, foster creativity, and remind students that caring for nature begins with *loving it* first.

Giving Back... Globally

While many of the practices in this chapter invite you to give back in small, personal, or local ways, there is also a wider world calling out for care. The challenges facing the earth are global in scale—climate change, deforestation, biodiversity loss, and pollution—but so too is the movement of people rising in love and action on behalf of the planet.

Wherever you are in the world, there are trusted and inspiring organisations working to heal the land, protect endangered species, restore forests, and advocate for a more sustainable future. These include tree-planting programs, wildlife protection efforts, conservation groups, and grassroots community projects that offer meaningful ways to contribute. You may wish to explore reputable global organisations such as WWF, One Tree Planted, The Nature Conservancy, or EarthDay.org, alongside Australian initiatives like Bush Heritage Australia, Greening Australia, and Seed Indigenous Youth Climate Network. Each of these organisations offers different ways to support—from donations to education to hands-on involvement.

But beyond the well-known, I also want to share a cause very close to my own heart—an initiative born from devotion, love for the land, and the desire to restore what has been lost. It's a project rooted in sacred intention, community empowerment, and environmental healing.

Green Sakthi – A Living Prayer for the Earth

Green Sakthi is an environmental initiative based at Sri Narayani Peedam, in Vellore, South India. This beautiful land, once stripped of its trees and scorched by the sun, has been lovingly transformed over the past 30 years into a flourishing oasis of green.

At the heart of this transformation is a deep reverence for nature and the guiding vision of Sri Sakthi Amma, whose love for the earth has inspired every tree planted, every sapling nurtured, and every life touched by this work.

Green Sakthi is not just a reforestation project—it is a living devotion. Over 2 million indigenous trees have been planted since its inception, cooling the land, bringing back rainfall, and restoring balance to the ecosystem.

The project now employs local women and men who care for over 100,000 saplings in the tree nursery and help reforest sacred groves and community lands with native and medicinal species. Sacred trees like kadamba, champa, sandalwood, mango, and jamun are being reintroduced, not just for their beauty, but for their healing, cultural, and spiritual significance.

Giving Back... Globally

But the work of Green Sakthi doesn't stop at planting trees. Their vision is wide-reaching—food forests, sustainable agriculture, community empowerment, and waste management are all part of their mission to heal both land and people. Organic fruits and vegetables grown through regenerative five-layer farming now goes towards feeding local community, visitors and workers.

The Green Sakthi Club is an engaging, hands-on program designed for students in grades 5 to 8, offering practical experiences in caring for the earth. From planting trees and harvesting vegetables to drawing nature and cleaning up litter, the club empowers young people to actively support the health of our planet. With a strong focus on learning and connecting children with nature, the program has already reached over 6,000 students—nurturing a new generation of environmentally conscious and earth-loving stewards.

I support Green Sakthi not only because of its environmental impact, but because it represents what *Wild Stillness* is all about—living in connection and care with the earth, giving with love, and allowing every small act to become a sacred offering. It reminds us that giving back to the earth can be an act of healing, of devotion, and of deep joy.

If this touches your heart too, I invite you to learn more or support this incredible work in any way that feels right for you. Together, we can help grow a future where nature thrives, communities flourish, and the sacred pulse of the earth is remembered and revered.

"Planting a tree is the greatest service you can do for Mother Earth, as every living being on this planet will benefit"

-Sri Sakthi Amma

A Moment of Reflection

Take a quiet moment to sit with what this chapter has stirred in you. Let these questions be gentle invitations, there is no right answer, only your truth in this moment.

What does giving back to the earth mean to you, personally? What small acts of care feel most aligned with your heart right now?

_____
_____
_____

Are there changes you'd like to make in your daily life—habits, choices, or rhythms—that reflect your love for the earth?

_____
_____
_____

What have you received from nature that you feel ready to honour or return?

_____
_____
_____

How have your feelings toward the natural world shifted throughout this journey?

_____
_____
_____

Do you feel complete with this chapter—for now? Has something softened or shifted in the way you relate to the earth and your place within it? Giving back doesn't end with a single action—it becomes part of how you live, how you choose, and how you care.

The next chapter invites you into a space of reflection and integration. A time to gather all that you've experienced—each breath, each practice, each moment of stillness and wonder—and gently weave it into the fabric of your daily life.

Chapter 10:
Your Wild Stillness Journey

In the quiet light of dawn, you step into the wild,
each breath a bridge between earth and soul.
In the hush of stillness, fragments of self align—
scattered pieces, slowly woven into one radiant tapestry.

Here, beneath ancient trees and open skies,
the pulse of the land echoes in your heart.
Every footstep, every whisper of wind,
guides you on a journey of gentle integration.

In this sacred communion of nature and being,
your wild spirit finds solace and unity.
Embrace the delicate dance of light and shadow,
where inner truth and wild stillness merge as one.

Welcome to your journey—ever unfolding, ever whole,
a path where every moment is a silent hymn
to the boundless, integrated beauty of your true self.

Integration & Your Wild Stillness Journey

As this journey through *Wild Stillness* nears its final pages, the true journey—the one that unfolds in your daily life—begins. This book has been an invitation, a doorway into deeper connection with nature, with yourself, and with the quiet wisdom that has always been present within and around you. Now, the question becomes: *How will you carry this forward?*

Integration is the process of weaving these experiences into the fabric of your life. It is not about rigidly following practices but about allowing the insights and moments of connection you've cultivated to gently shape how you move through the world. Maybe you've discovered the power of stillness beneath a tree, or felt the sacred rhythm of your breath mirrored in the wind. Perhaps you've awakened to the simple joy of watching the sky shift at dusk, or felt a deep knowing in your heart that you are not separate from nature—you *are* nature.

What follows are simple suggestions and gentle guidance on how to keep this connection alive—how to let nature's wisdom infuse your daily rhythms, how to continue deepening your awareness, and how to live in a way that honours both your inner stillness and the wild beauty of the world around you.

Your journey doesn't end here. It continues with every step you take upon the earth, every breath of fresh air, every moment of presence you choose to embrace. The wild stillness is always waiting. It is always here. And so are you.

Making Nature a Priority

Just as we make time for the gym, for work, for family, or for daily tasks, we can also choose to make time for being in nature. Our well-being deserves to be a priority—not as an afterthought, but as something essential to how we live. Committing even 15 to 20 minutes a day to immersing ourselves in the natural world can have profound effects on our physical, emotional, and mental health. If stepping into nature daily isn't an option, then carving out an hour on the weekend to visit a local park, forest, or coastline can provide a deeper reset.

The key is consistency. Like any practice, the more we engage with it, the more natural it becomes. Just as strengthening a muscle requires repeated effort, deepening our connection with nature takes practice. At first, it might feel unfamiliar to sit in stillness under a tree, to walk slowly with awareness, or to listen deeply to the sounds around us. But over time, the benefits become undeniable. We begin to feel more at ease, more connected, and more present—not just in nature, but in every part of our lives.

This is not about adding another obligation to your to-do list. It is about choosing *you*. Choosing to invest in your own well-being. Choosing to step outside, breathe deeply, and reconnect—not because you *have* to, but because you *deserve* to. The more you prioritise these moments, the more they will shape the way you move through the world. And in doing so, you won't just be improving your own life—you will be bringing a calmer, more present, more grounded version of yourself into everything you do and everyone you meet.

Going Deeper

Once we begin this journey—returning to nature, to presence, to ourselves—something remarkable starts to happen. We begin to *notice more*. Not just the beauty of the world around us, but the subtle truths within. Stillness sharpens our awareness, and awareness reveals what was once hidden beneath the noise of everyday life.

At first, this noticing may bring us more joy. We see colours more vividly, feel the breeze more tenderly, hear the song of a bird as if for the first time. But in time, we also begin to notice other things—the patterns in our thoughts, the tension in our bodies, the way we react, speak, or hold ourselves in the world. Sometimes, this noticing can startle us. We may find ourselves asking, *Do I really act that way? Do I truly believe what I just said? Is that who I want to be?*

These are not easy questions—but they are powerful ones. And they mark the beginning of the deepest transformation of all: the journey of becoming more aligned with our truth. Of living in a way that reflects our heart, our values, and our connection with all life.

This is the lifelong path. There is no end point, only layers of awakening. And the more time we spend in awareness, presence, and stillness, the more clearly we see—not just the world, but ourselves. This clarity becomes our greatest tool for healing, for change, for liberation.

It takes courage to see ourselves clearly. To face what's uncomfortable, and to begin to shift. But what a gift it is. To no longer move through life asleep, but awake. Aware. Whole.

This is the gift of going deeper. And it is always waiting.

Following Your Heart Forward

As you look back over the pages and practices of *Wild Stillness*, take a quiet moment to notice—*what called to you most?* Was it the softness of breath in the trees, the spark of creativity in art with natural materials, the sensory immersion of barefoot walks and birdsong, or the deep fulfilment of giving back to the earth?

These heart-pulls are not random. They are signposts. Gentle whispers from your inner knowing, pointing you toward what nourishes you most. This is your compass—unique, intuitive, and wise.

There's no need to follow every practice or revisit every chapter. Simply notice what made you feel most alive, most grounded, most at peace. Let that guide your next steps. You may choose to deepen your connection through one focus—like breathwork in nature, or ritual and sacred art—or you might continue to move gently between different aspects, trusting your rhythm to shift with the seasons.

There is no right way, only *your* way. And when you follow what lights up your heart, presence becomes effortless, and the path unfolds naturally beneath your feet. Let your joy lead. Let your wonder guide. The journey forward is yours.

Ways to Continue Your Wild Stillness Journey

1. Make Nature a Daily Practice, No Matter Where You Are

You don't need to be deep in the wilderness to stay connected to the natural world. The sky, the wind, the trees, and the seasons exist wherever you are. Make time each day—even just a few minutes—to step outside, breathe deeply, and notice the living world around you.

☽ Reflection: What are simple ways I can invite nature into my daily life?

_____
_____

2. Keep a Nature Journal & Record Your Inner and Outer Landscapes

Journaling is a powerful way to deepen your awareness and integrate your experiences. Write about the changes you notice in the natural world—the shift of the seasons, the behaviour of birds, the colour of the sky at different times of day. But also write about your inner world—how being in nature makes you feel, what emotions arise, what wisdom the land seems to whisper.

☽ Reflection: How does my inner landscape shift when I spend time in nature? What patterns do I notice?

_____
_____

3. Return to the Practices That Resonated Most

Throughout this journey, certain practices may have touched you more deeply than others. Maybe it was sitting in stillness beneath a tree, creating ephemeral art, or heart-opening rituals with the elements. Return to the practices that called to you. Let them evolve and become part of your personal way of being with the world.

☽ Reflection: Which Wild Stillness practices felt the most meaningful to me? How can I revisit them in a way that fits into my life?

_____
_____

4. Honour the Cycles of Nature (and Your Own Cycles Too)

Nature moves in rhythms—day and night, the waxing and waning moon, the changing of the seasons. When we align our lives with these natural cycles, we feel more balanced and connected. Notice how your energy shifts with the time of day or the seasons. Honour these changes by adjusting your routines, creating small rituals to welcome each season, or simply pausing to acknowledge where you are in the cycle of life.

☽ Reflection: How do I experience the cycles of nature in my own body, emotions, and energy?

_____
_____

5. Live with Reverence—For Yourself, Others, and the Earth

Reverence is about seeing the sacred in all things—not just in grand landscapes, but in the small, everyday moments. It's about treating yourself, others, and the earth with care. Carry this awareness into your actions: walk gently on the land, express gratitude for the earth's gifts, tread lightly in the choices you make, and cultivate kindness in your interactions. Living with reverence transforms the way you move through the world.

🌙 **Reflection:** How can I bring more presence and care into my relationship with myself, others, and the earth?

_____
_____

6. Be a Guardian of the Wild—Protect What You Love

The more deeply we connect with nature, the more we feel called to protect it. Whether it's through small personal actions—reducing waste, choosing sustainable living, supporting conservation—or through simply inspiring others to rekindle their own connection with the wild, you become a guardian of what you love.

🌙 **Reflection:** How can I give back to nature in a way that feels meaningful to me?

_____
_____

7. Create a Simple Reminder

When life moves fast, it's easy to forget to pause. Place small reminders around your home—a leaf on your desk, a shell by your bedside, a nature-inspired affirmation on your phone wallpaper. Let these symbols call you back to the present moment.

🌙 Try This: Choose a "nature anchor" to keep nearby—a stone, feather, or twig. Hold it when you feel overwhelmed and let it remind you to slow down. What object speaks to you?

_____
_____

8. Be Gentle With Yourself

There is no "failing" at Wild Stillness. Even if you haven't connected with nature for weeks or months, the earth is still here, waiting for you with open arms. The trees, the rivers, the wind—none of them hold expectations for you. They simply invite you back when you are ready.

🌙 Try This: Whisper to yourself, I am allowed to pause. I am always welcome back. Or write your own.

_____
_____

Acknowledgements

Dear Wild Stillness Traveller,

This book has been shaped by stillness, breath, beauty, and the quiet companionship of the natural world. But it was also shaped—deeply—by people.

To my beloved Guru, Sri Sakthi Amma Narayani, whose presence and teachings have lit the path of my life with love, purpose, and service—thank you. Every word in these pages is an offering from that light.

To the land itself—especially the bushland of the Adelaide Hills, which has held me through uncertainty, joy, clarity, and becoming. You have been my teacher, my refuge, and my home.

To my family, for your patience, love, and belief—even when I disappeared into long silences with pen in hand or feet on the forest floor.

To my friends and soul companions, for walking this journey beside me and reminding me of the beauty in both wildness and stillness.

To the children, educators, and fellow seekers I've taught and walked with over the years—your presence, questions, and open hearts have inspired and shaped much of what this book became.

And to you, the reader—thank you for opening these pages, for slowing down enough to listen, and for walking gently with your breath, your heart, and the earth. This journey is as much yours as it is mine.

I would truly love to hear how this journey has unfolded for you. Your reflections—whether joyful or tender, certain or uncertain—are most welcome. Feel free to reach out and share your story with me. You can email me at: centreformindfuleducation@gmail.com.

Wherever you are in your journey, you belong here.

With my deepest gratitude and love,

Jan Carey

Sources of Inspiration

The words and practices within *Wild Stillness* have grown slowly, shaped by my own lived experiences in nature and nurtured by the teachings of many wise beings—both human and more-than-human.

While most of this book has flowed from my personal journey, I want to honour the voices, traditions, and texts that have offered guidance, perspective, and quiet encouragement along the way.

If something in these pages spoke to you deeply, you may wish to explore these sources for yourself:

- *The Upanishads* - translations and commentaries on ancient Indian wisdom
- *The Power of Now* - Eckhart Tolle's teachings on presence and awareness
- *Braiding Sweetgrass* - Robin Wall Kimmerer's beautiful weaving of Indigenous knowledge and ecological science
- *The Hidden Life of Trees* - Peter Wohlleben's insights into the intelligence of forests
- *Connect with the Divine* series, teachings and blessings of Sri Sakthi Amma Narayani
- Mindfulness practices shared by Thich Nhat Hanh
- Forest Bathing and Nature Therapy (Shinrin-Yoku) traditions from Japan

I'm grateful for the deep roots of these traditions, and for the many quiet teachers—seen and unseen—who continue to remind me that nature is not outside us, but *part* of us.

This list is not complete, but it is offered in the spirit of reverence and sharing. May these sources support your journey, just as they have supported mine.

The Wild Stillness Journey
108 nature-based practices to awaken presence and peace

Practice Index

Returning to Presence — Pg

1. Stillness Sit — 18
2. Rooted Feet — 19
3. Panoramic Presence — 20
4. Water Reflection — 21
5. A Closer look — 22
6. Birdwatching Presence — 23
7. Tree connection — 24
8. Evening Contemplation — 25
9. Seasonal Change — 26
10. Memory Walk — 27
11. Mindful Pause — 28
12. Embodied Presence — 29

The Breath of the Earth

13. Sunrise Breath — 34
14. Breath of the Land — 35
15. Tree Breathing — 36
16. Wave Breathing — 37
17. Wind Breathing — 38
18. Mountain Breathing — 39
19. Moon Breathing — 40
20. Stillness Between Breaths — 41
21. Cyclic Breathing — 42
22. Full Circle Breathing — 43
23. Gifting Your Breath — 44
24. Wild Breath — 45

Open Your Heart to the Wild — Pg

25. Gratitude Trail Walk — 52
26. Loving-Kindness — 53
27. Flower of forgiveness — 54
28. Sunset of Love — 55
29. Forgiveness Flow — 56
30. Wild Love Letters — 57
31. Gratitude Circle — 58
32. Earth's Heartbeat — 59
33. Birdsong of Joy — 60
34. Rock Patience — 61
35. Sun's Embrace — 62
36. Nature's Beauty — 63

Awaken the Senses

37. Nature's Symphony — 68
38. Scented Wander — 69
39. Barefoot connection — 70
40. Herbal touch — 71
41. Soil grounding — 72
42. Treasure Hunt — 73
43. Earth's Vibration — 74
44. Scented Memory — 75
45. Water Whisper — 76
46. Nature's Taste — 77
47. Wind's Caress — 78
48. Acoustic Meditation — 79

Create with the Land	**Pg**	**Leaving No Trace**	**Pg**
49. Mindful Rock Painting	84	81. Gratitude Mandala	124
50. Leaf Breathing Art	85	82. Breathing Brushstrokes	125
51. Sky Doodling	86	83. Stone Stacking	126
52. Shadow drawing	87	84. Zen Sand Designs	127
53. Nature Rubbings	88	85. Nature Collage	128
54. Soundscape Sketching	89	86. Driftwood Mandalas	129
55. Calming Petals	90	87. Mud Finger Painting	130
56. Texture Sketch	91	88. Sand Mandala	131
57. One-Line Drawing	92	89. Twig Sculptures	132
58. Sunset Silhouette	93	90. Chalk Drawings	133
59. Stillness Silhouettes	94	91. Flower Petal Collage	134
60. Dew Drop Drawing	95	92. Nature Shadow Art	135
61. Sit Spot Sketching	96		
62. Tactile Clay Creations	97	**Sacred Nature, Sacred Self**	
63. Cloud Shape Creations	98		
64. Puddle Painting	99	93. Sacred Heart Altar	142
65. Wishing Stones	100	94. Sunrise Greeting	143
66. Walking Doodles	101	95. Tree Spirit Meditation	144
67. Echo Art	102	96. Water Blessing	145
68. Fossil imprint	103	97. Earth Meditation	146
		98. Sacred Nature Walk	147
Storytelling with Nature		99. Moon Journal	148
		100. Elemental Offering	149
69. Leaf Collage Narrative	108	101. Rainfall Blessing	150
70. Pebble Stories	109	102. Prayer Flags	151
71. Rock Portraits	110	103. Silent Solitude	152
72. Soundscape Storytelling	111	104. Seasonal Celebration	153
73. Letter to Nature	112	105. Firelight Reflection	154
74. Wildflower Poem	113	106. Nature Reading Ritual	155
75. Animal Encounter	114	107. Stargazing Reverie	156
76. Free-Flow Writing	115	108. Sunset Reflection	157
77. Night Sky Narrative	116		
78. Personal Totem	117		
79. Time Capsule Story	118		
80. Nature Dialogue	119		

Wild Reflections

date:

Wild Reflections

date:

About The Author – Jan Carey

Jan Carey is a mindfulness educator, writer, and nature-based practitioner with a background in education and over a decade of experience guiding others in mindful awareness, self-inquiry, and creative exploration. Her work draws from a rich integration of formal mindfulness training, classroom teaching, and deep personal practice.

Having taught in both mainstream and alternative education settings, she brings a grounded, accessible approach to mindfulness that is both practical and heart-centred. Her teachings are rooted not only in theory, but in a life lived intentionally—immersed in presence, simplicity, and connection with the natural world.

Jan lives on a 46-acre bushland property in the Adelaide Hills, South Australia, where the rhythms of nature guide her daily life and creative process. Surrounded by gum trees, kangaroos, and birdsong, she finds inspiration in the quiet wisdom of the land and brings this deep connection into her writing and teaching. Her personal practices—spanning breathwork, nature meditation, creativity, and contemplative walking—are woven into every aspect of her life and work.

A long-time student of Eastern spiritual traditions, she regularly spends extended periods in India at her Guru's ashram, engaging in spiritual study, seva (selfless service), and inner reflection. This immersion has brought a depth and sacredness to her understanding of mindfulness as more than a practice—an ongoing way of being.

In both her teaching and writing, Jan is committed to authenticity, simplicity, and offering others a genuine path back to themselves. This book, *Wild Stillness: A Journey into Mindfulness, Creativity, and the Sacred Wisdom of Nature*, is a heartfelt expression of this path—inviting readers to slow down, listen deeply, and reconnect with the beauty of the natural world and the stillness within.

About Centre for Mindful Education

The Centre for Mindful Education is dedicated to supporting mindful, creative, and nature-connected approaches to learning and wellbeing. Founded by educator and mindfulness practitioner Jan Carey, the Centre creates resources and programs that nurture presence, emotional awareness, and inner stillness—blending modern mindfulness with timeless wisdom and a deep reverence for the natural world.

Centre for Mindful Education
centreformindfuleducation@gmail.com
www.centreformindfuleducation.com
facebook.com/centreformindfuleducation

www.ingramcontent.com/pod-product-compliance
Lightning Source LLC
Chambersburg PA
CBHW061128170426
43209CB00014B/1704